W9-BYA-321

OPERATION IRAQI FREEDOM

OPERATION
IRAQI FREEDOM

NBC NEWS

Written by Marc Kusnetz;
William M. Arkin; General Montgomery Meigs, retired;
and Neal Shapiro

Andrews McMeel
Publishing
Kansas City

OPERATION IRAQI FREEDOM

Copyright © 2003 by National Broadcasting Company, Inc. All rights reserved. Printed in the United States of America. No part of this book may be used or reproduced in any manner whatsoever without written permission except in the case of reprints in the context of reviews. For information, write Andrews McMeel Publishing, an Andrews McMeel Universal company, 4520 Main Street, Kansas City, Missouri 64111.

03 04 05 06 07 RR3 10 9 8 7 6 5 4 3 2 1

Library of Congress Cataloging-in-Publication Data on file

Design by Holly Camerlinck

Photoediting by Leora Kahn

A portion of the proceeds from this book will be donated to charity.

Attention: Schools and Businesses

Andrews McMeel books are available at quantity discounts with bulk purchase for educational, business, or sales promotional use. For information, please write to: Special Sales Department, Andrews McMeel Publishing, 4520 Main Street, Kansas City, Missouri 64111

Contents

FROM THE CHAIRMAN

On December 7, 1941, the fateful day that propelled the United States into World War II, David Sarnoff, chairman of NBC, sent this message via radiogram to President Franklin D. Roosevelt: "All of our facilities and personnel are ready and at your instant service. We await your commands."

As a chapter in military history, the bombing of Pearl Harbor was nothing like the events in Iraq that began the evening of March 19, 2003. The circumstances and the times were very different, and Sarnoff's spontaneous gesture of support would be misinterpreted today. Nonetheless, as an event that mobilized the men and women of NBC, there are parallels. In both cases, NBC's news and broadcast operations professionals threw themselves headlong into a cause that has no greater importance to the people of a free nation: reporting the actions and activities of the United States military, as fully and as accurately as possible.

Sarnoff was charged with delivering a healthy bottom line to the shareholders of RCA, NBC's corporate parent. More than sixty years later, it's my job to do the same for GE and its shareholders. For that reason, although news has always been at the very heart of what we do at NBC, I take no special pleasure in authorizing our news division to boost its spending by millions of dollars. But with the unequivocal backing of Jeff Immelt, GE's CEO, I took a deep breath and did what I had to do. When it became clear that the nation was headed into a war, I told Neal Shapiro, president of NBC News, to spend whatever he thought necessary to cover the conflict. I think my exact words were "Neal, spend what you need, not a penny more, not a penny less."

Perhaps I inherited from Sarnoff a belief that our business has attached to it imperatives that transcend any financial reckoning of success. Over its seventy-seven-year history, NBC has developed a unique relationship with the American people. We reach the citizens of this nation with remarkable immediacy and impact. Even in our age of multimedia saturation, we are overwhelmingly who the public turns to in times of crisis or emergency. In fact, if you are reading these words, there is a good chance you are one of the millions of American television viewers who watched with awe and fascination as David Bloom shared with us what it was like to be part of the 3rd ID convoy, rumbling north toward Baghdad in the middle of a sandstorm.

The reach and power of broadcasting bestow on us a heightened responsibility, and it is my job now, as it was David Sarnoff's in an earlier era, to ensure that we meet this challenge in a way that we will look back on with pride. That is certainly the case with our coverage of Operation Iraqi Freedom, which marks a high point in the long tradition of excellence of NBC News.

So, just as Sarnoff sent dozens of reporters and technicians across the globe to report on World War II, we dispatched scores to Afghanistan, Turkey, Kuwait, and Iraq. We had correspondents on aircraft carriers and in armored vehicles, at the Pentagon and at Central Command, reporting from the White House and the State Department. Wherever we needed to be to get the story, we were there.

Much has changed since 1941 in the world of broadcasting and the waging of war. During World War II, American citizens heard tinny voices coming to them from Europe and Asia via shortwave radio. For Operation Iraqi Freedom, we deployed an arsenal of equipment using technologies that could not have been imagined then, enabling us to bring you vivid images and sound instantaneously from battlefields half a world away.

The nature of broadcasting has evolved, and so has the relationship between the press and the military. More than six hundred reporters were embedded with the troops during this conflict: journalists eating, sleeping, and moving in concert with their assigned combat units. Among the most prominent were a handful of intrepid reporters from NBC News and MSNBC, who traveled with the support of a small contingent of staff photographers, producers, and engineers. This book shares with you the remarkable stories of these courageous men and women, who served the nation not as soldiers but as journalists.

In 1938, as Hitler's armies invaded Austria, a blanket order was sent by radiogram to NBC's correspondents in Europe: "Be there and get the news!" Now, as then, the people of NBC News go where they have to go, regardless of hardship and danger, to bring you the news that a democratic society needs and deserves. That's the enduring spirit of NBC News. And that's the spirit that animates the following pages.

Bob Wright

BOB WRIGHT
VICE CHAIRMAN AND EXECUTIVE OFFICER, GE,
AND CHAIRMAN AND CEO, NBC

FOREWORD

BY TOM BROKAW

President Bush's decision to commit American forces to war in Iraq came as no surprise. The prospect of war had been with us for months during spirited debates at the United Nations, in the Congress, and on the streets of cities around the world. Nonetheless, it was a sobering moment for the nation, because no presidential action is as consequential as the decision to go to war.

For the journalists of NBC News and other news organizations, it was to be a different kind of war. It would be possible to provide live coverage—or coverage that was only slightly delayed—directly from the battlefield onto television screens throughout the world, including the Arab world, where technical and political constraints had previously discouraged coverage of unfolding news events.

At NBC News we had spent several months preparing for what we knew would be one of the most demanding assignments since the terrorist attacks of 9/11. Our reporters and producers who would be embedded with military units on the front lines were sent to military training schools to learn the rudiments of survival in combat.

In New York, Washington, London, Doha, Kuwait City, Amman, and Tel Aviv, extra personnel were brought in and special production techniques were tested repeatedly. We assembled a team of retired high-ranking military specialists from all branches of the services to serve as consultants and expert commentators.

It was all in place that first night when President Bush, acting on urgent intelligence from a spy on the ground in Baghdad, decided to move up the timetable in the hopes of taking out Saddam Hussein and his two sons with a preemptive air strike against a leadership compound where they were thought to be spending the night.

Suddenly, the war was under way. NBC News correspondent David Bloom and his team were moving north with the 3rd Infantry Division. Correspondents Chip Reid and Kerry Sanders moved out with the Marines. Dana Lewis was reporting in from the 101st Airborne and Brian Williams kept us apprised of missile attacks launched at Kuwait. Fred Francis was covering the Kurds in northern Iraq, and George Lewis was tracking the on-again, off-again role of the Turks right next door. In Washington, Jim Miklaszewski, Andrea Mitchell, Pete Williams, David Gregory, and Campbell Brown were on the air from the Departments of Defense,

State, and Justice, along with the White House. Other correspondents and production teams were assigned to military bases around the nation to cover the war on the home front.

The New York control rooms were humming with incoming feeds for all NBC News programs, while across the Hudson River in New Jersey, MSNBC and CNBC were covering the war and its effects around the clock. It was all going rapidly but smoothly as the animated maps unfolded stylishly on the screens, and reporters from the *New York Times,* the *Washington Post,* our British television partner ITN, and *National Geographic Explorer* came on the air with urgent updates.

Then, on the third day of the war, Nancy Chamberlain, mother of a U.S. Marine, gave us all pause. She had a poignant cautionary note for us about the real meaning of war beyond the television images. Mrs. Chamberlain's son, Marine Captain Jay Aubin, had just been killed when his Sea Knight helicopter crashed during a nighttime sandstorm.

We managed to reach her on the telephone at her home near Waterbury, Maine, after the death of her son was confirmed. In a soft but determined voice she described Jay's devotion to the Marines and his instruction that if something happened, the family should remember that he died doing what he absolutely loved and believed in. She went on to describe his wife and the two children he left behind, her grandchildren.

As I was concluding the interview, expressing the condolences of NBC News and the nation, Mrs. Chamberlain interrupted me to say, "Mr. Brokaw, may I make a point?" Then, speaking of the war coverage, she said, "I truly admire what all the network news and news technologies are doing today to bring it into our homes. But for the mothers and wives who are out there watching, it is murder. It's heartbreak. We can't leave the television. Every tank, every helicopter, 'Is that my son?' And I just need you to be aware that technology is great. But there are moms, there are dads, there are wives who are suffering because of this. That's why I'm doing this."

By that time I was fighting for control of my own emotions because this eloquent woman, who had just lost her son, was performing such an important public service for those of us in journalism and those who were watching.

War is about big decisions, hard truths, and deceptions. But most of all, it is about dying and surviving and taking care of each other. In this account of the work of NBC News during Operation Iraqi Freedom, you will read about all of that and more. As you absorb what we witnessed and what we learned, remember the words of Nancy Chamberlain, a mother who in her grief served the nation as surely as her Marine son served the nation and gave his life.

INTRODUCTION

BY GENERAL MONTGOMERY MEIGS, RETIRED

Operation Iraqi Freedom, the U.S. campaign to unseat the government of Saddam Hussein in Iraq, represented a major step in the development of American joint military operations. The campaign had four phases: deployment and preparation, initial attack, capture of Baghdad and regime change, and reconstruction and peacekeeping. In every phase except the last, coalition forces had tremendous success, integrating capabilities of the different service branches, national intelligence systems, and special operations units with unprecedented discipline and skill. In addition, the increased operational synergy gained from information-age technologies made a significant difference on and above the battlefield. In spite of these successes, however, the national commitment to reconstruction and peacekeeping remains uncertain.

The campaign's first phase actually started many months before the initial strikes on the evening of March 19, 2003. Under Operations Northern and Southern Watch in the years leading up to the war, American pilots patrolled airspace in the U.N.-mandated no-fly zones over large portions of Iraq. Initially, pilots played cat and mouse with Iraqi air defenders, but after Operation Desert Fox in

December 1998, the operations against Iraqi air defenses and communications became methodical. By early 2003, American and British pilots had not only made significant headway in disrupting Iraqi command and control, but their commanders and intelligence operators had also developed unprecedented familiarity with available targets in a larger campaign.

On the ground, soldiers and Marines expanded their knowledge of the operational environment. In the successive training missions Intrinsic Action and Eager Mace, Army and Marine units rotated into Kuwait, took over equipment positioned in advance there, and maneuvered in the desert. Staff teams developed terrain studies, improved their understanding of the enemy order of battle, and refined likely courses of action. In military history, seldom has a force had the opportunity to study an opponent as thoroughly as U.S. Central Command and its component commands did in Iraq.

During the deployment phase, additional Army and Marine equipment moved into place by sea, Centcom and its component headquarters held exercises in the region and at home to validate war plans, and advanced command and control systems were constructed in Kuwait and Qatar. Faced with the necessity of deploying forces through only one port and one airbase in Kuwait, U.S. leaders made sure the campaign did not launch from a standing start. The Army's 4th Infantry Division packed its heavy equipment on ships and sent them to the eastern Mediterranean in anticipation of Turkish approval to use its territory and airspace as assembly areas for a northern offensive into Iraq. The Navy doubled its carrier force at sea, committing five carrier battle groups to the campaign.

After months of preparation, forces on the ground, at sea, and in the air were in place; they knew their enemy and the environment in which they would fight. Iraqi Freedom was not a "come as you are" war. In the months before March, diplomats conducted frenzied negotiations to enlist allies and gain U.N. support. French, German, and Belgian resistance to the U.S. strategic intent frustrated a NATO-derived coalition and left scars that may see the unraveling of the alliance as we know it.

As the decision to attack drew closer, the threat of weapons of mass destruction created tension for ground troops. Soldiers and Marines in assembly areas and airmen on bases sweated out the danger of missile-borne chemical attacks. They withstood frequent alarms requiring frantic donning of chemical suits and masks and long, anxious stays in hot, crowded bunkers. Men and women at sea agonized over mines and the likelihood of shore-to-ship missile attacks. All deployed personnel remained continuously wary of terrorist attacks, but frustration and inactivity bred determination. In the words of embedded NBC journalist David Bloom reporting from the 3rd Infantry Division, "These nine hundred soldiers will be the first to cross over into Iraq. They're eager to go."

The operational strategy used in Iraqi Freedom does not represent a departure from military history. Napoléon's turning movement at Ulm, the so-called blitzkrieg in 1940 against France, and Bradley's breakout from Normandy and advance across the Seine were all based on similar concepts: Control the point of attack to continually surprise your enemy and confront him with accelerating events that he finds shocking and incredible. Cut his means of communication with his units and his logistic system so he cannot command or refit his forces. Bypass the bulk of his combat power. Then, by rapidly destroying units in contact at the point of attack, undermine the morale of his fighting outfits.

For all of its similarities to previous campaigns, however, Iraqi Freedom was unique in benefiting from information-age technology that enhanced the commanders' ability to achieve those effects. In today's operational arena, if enemy elements move on the battlefield in anything but small groups at night, they can be located by sensors, recorded, catalogued, and portrayed in a coordinated operational picture of the battle that is available to leaders in ships, wings, brigades, and at the nation's capital. Decisions about where to place the point of attack on the ground and what formation to target from the air can be made in almost real time.

The initial attacks on March 19 stemmed from just such a technological advantage. Given a break in intelligence, President Bush ordered a change of plan and authorized a strike on a Baghdad residence where Saddam and his two sons were reported to be present. Centcom commander General Tommy Franks soon shifted the plan again. The original concept called for launching the attack on the ground on March 22 after the air operation had begun. Franks and his ground commanders accelerated the land assault, beginning the offensive with almost no preparatory strikes from the air.

On March 20, three distinct but integrated campaigns fired into action. In northern and western Iraq, Special Operations Forces sought to neutralize the threat of Iraqi Scud missiles fired into Israel to provoke a response by the Israeli Defense Force, which would surely inflame the Arab world. These forces worked in Kurdish areas to tie down Iraqi divisions and keep the Kurds from launching their own offensive, and, in the early hours Iraqi time, they subsequently attacked the base of Ansar al-Islam and the Zarqawi group, terrorist organizations linked to al-Qaeda. In the south, Navy SEALs raided targets on the Faw peninsula in the Persian Gulf. Following these assaults, British and U.S. Marines began their offensive on Umm Qasr with the objective of taking Basra, Iraq's second largest city and the center of the Shi'ite population in the south.

To ensure that his forces quickly gained air superiority, chief air commander Lieutenant General Michael Moseley sought to destroy Iraq's ability to contest its airspace, as well as its communication networks and regime command centers. Air teams from the Air Force, Navy, Marines, the Royal Air Force, and the Australian Air Force focused first on shattering the integrity of Iraqi air defenses and then moved on to destroy various regime targets and take out any delivery means for chemical weapons.

On the ground, V Corps moved quickly to counter its most difficult challenge. Lieutenant General William S. Wallace knew that any crossing of the Euphrates River and its canal system could be treacherous, and he wanted to avoid a direct crossing that would be vulnerable to attack by

chemical weapons. Feinting a march between the Euphrates and Tigris Rivers and bypassing enemy forces at Nasiriyah and Samawah, the 3rd ID headed into the desert on the west bank of the Euphrates and raced for the Karbala gap, about fifty miles southwest of Baghdad. Wallace wanted to slip around the flank of the Republican Guard units in front of the city, surprising the Iraqi command with an attack that was earlier than they believed possible and from an unexpected direction. Maintaining surprise and operational initiative meant holding the river line, covering the Corps' lines of communication back to Kuwait, and cloaking the advance of forces through the western desert. By March 23, V Corps was racing into the vicinity of Karbala. In four days, it traveled over 260 miles as the crow flies but considerably more on the unimproved roads and tracks that made up the line of the march.

The Marines attacked Basra and simultaneously crossed the Euphrates at Nasiriyah, moving through the central Mesopotamian Valley to Baghdad and feinting toward Diwaniyah before driving west on Highway 27 to assault the Iraqi capital from the southeast. This operation relied on a quick crossing of the southern Euphrates with its complex system of waterways and then a rapid advance toward Baghdad.

When the Turkish Parliament refused to allow the United States to open a northern front, General Franks decided on March 22 to move the equipment of the 4th ID from the eastern Mediterranean through the Suez Canal and commit it from the south. The 4th ID would not get into the fight until the very end of the campaign, but the division's readiness to stage into Turkey may have kept two Republican Guard divisions around Kirkuk and Mosul out of the fight for Baghdad. Lieutenant General Dave McKiernan, combined land force commander, now had to conduct the ground campaign without the most technically advanced division in the Army.

In the north and west, Special Operations Forces operated in secrecy; their activities still remain undisclosed. However, the Iraqis were not able to launch a single missile at Israel. The combination of Special Operations and precision weaponry delivered from the air wreaked havoc on Iraqi capabilities. The air operation quickly disposed of the country's integrated air defense, and no Iraqi aircraft rose to contest its airspace. As a result, early in the campaign Lieutenant General Moseley was able to focus his effort on the Republican Guard and continue attacking Iraqi military and regime targets at will.

From March 25 to March 30 the ground "pause" took place. It actually involved a wide range of intense activity accomplished in the very teeth of raging sandstorms, increasing heat, and the threat of chemical attack. Wallace leapfrogged units along his flank to protect the Euphrates crossings and, once the situation was stable, replaced 101st Airborne Division brigades to have them ready for the Baghdad assault. Simultaneously, V Corps weakened Republican Guard units defending crossing sites northeast of Karbala and approaches to the city. Wallace also checked aggressive Fedayeen attacks on his supply lines, now more than three hundred miles long. There is no question that resupply and retrieving, and refitting broken down combat vehicles, became critical at this point, forcing General Franks to release an 82nd Airborne Division brigade from his reserve to V Corps, assisted by part of the 2nd Armored Cavalry, a light reconnaissance regiment.

The Marines assumed responsibility for reducing resistance in Nasiriyah and encountered tough street fighting. The 1st Marine Division began its movement toward Numaniyah on the Tigris, while in Basra, British Royal Marines and a brigade of the British 1st Armored Division found itself in a conventional struggle to subdue a large urban area. Heavy nose-to-nose combat took place in Nasiriyah, Najaf, Samawah, Diwaniyah, and the approaches to Basra. In the north, the 173rd Airborne Brigade parachuted at night into the Bashur airfield in the Kurdish sector to reinforce the efforts of the Special Forces.

By March 30 at the end of the pause, McKiernan, Wallace, Marine component commander Lieutenant General Jim Conway, and Moseley had set the conditions for the final advance on Baghdad, and the Kurdish area remained stable. Even with the absence of the 4th ID, air superiority allowed Special Operators and the 173rd to move on Mosul and Kirkuk with Kurdish Peshmerga irregulars. The air operation and attacks by Army helicopters and artillery savaged the Republican Guard's Medina division in front of Baghdad and its Baghdad division that lay in wait for the Marines. Later, when the Hammurabi and al-Nida divisions attempted to move out of the city and the Adnan and Nebuchadnezzar divisions moved south to join the fight, they suffered similar attrition.

As the second phase ended, V Corps was in position at the Karbala gap just outside the range of chemical weapons and ready for the final assault on the capital. The 1st Marine Expeditionary Force had opened the way to the Tigris and to Baghdad over two hundred miles away. British forces had surrounded Basra; its fall became inevitable.

Ground forces were spread thin. With the operational agility of his land units and the firepower available from his air operation, General Franks could maintain the initiative, seize Baghdad, and topple the regime. But doubts emerged about whether he could do all that and simultaneously initiate peacekeeping activities. As Centcom fought the battle for Baghdad, its success would depend on seizing seats of power, putting down Ba'athist attempts to subvert reconstruction, and immediately improving security and services in Iraqi communities. One troubling development did not augur well for the future: The Shi'ite community did not welcome coalition forces with open arms. The Shi'ites remembered being left alone with Saddam's henchmen in 1991, and they remained in the shadows waiting for events to unfold.

On March 31, Jim Miklaszewski reported, "It appears today that American ground forces are making significant progress." The third phase of the campaign had begun. In two weeks the conventional military part of the war would be over.

By now, the air operation had directed more than 60 percent of its sorties in support of Army, Marine, or Special Forces Ground Operations and 14 percent against regime command and control targets. Space-based sensors and airborne platforms like JSTARS, U-2, Predator, and Global Hawk showed Iraqi conventional forces to U.S. headquarters during running battles. Enemy formations were targeted continuously by air, artillery, and attack helicopters. On April 7, intelligence seemed to locate Saddam at a restaurant in Baghdad's Mansour neighborhood. The Air Force diverted a B-1 bomber from other objectives to attack the building, with indeterminate results. But the flexibility and responsiveness of air assets and

the ability to place bombs within feet of projected targets represented a significant new capability in U.S. joint operations.

On the ground, V Corps fought its way through remnants of the Medina division and attacks by Fedayeen and paramilitaries to the outskirts of Baghdad, first seizing Saddam International airport on April 4 Baghdad time. Fortunately, the Iraqis did not respond with chemical attacks. After a stiff fight for the airport and a series of reconnaissance raids on the city, on April 6 the 3rd ID moved brigades to the bridges over the Tigris in central Baghdad and on Highway 1 northwest of the city. Fighting continued for several days as the units consolidated their positions in central Baghdad and to the north. Also on April 6, Britain's 3rd battalion of the Parachute Regiment cleared the old quarter of Basra on foot.

Meanwhile, the Marines crossed the Tigris at Numaniyah and forced their way up Highway 6. Having fought their way through remnants of the Baghdad and al-Nida Republican Guard divisions and crossed the Diyala River, on April 9 they reached Firdos circle in downtown Baghdad and, with the help of Iraqi citizens, pulled down the large statue of Saddam there. Ominously, looting began immediately in the city, but the Iraqi military was no longer a factor. On April 14, the Pentagon declared that major military operations had ended.

The war was effectively over, but hostilities continued in various areas. In Fallujah west of Baghdad and other areas such as Amarah in the south, remnants of Iraqi forces targeted U.S. troops. In Basra and Baghdad, the enemy destroyed key infrastructures in the power system, aided by criminals who cut down power lines to retrieve copper for sale in Iran. These efforts damaged an already overtaxed electric grid. Looting also took a toll on water-pumping stations, power plants, and warehouses holding vital spare parts. Looters even ravaged hospitals and Iraqi government offices responsible for civilian utilities.

On April 8, the Office for Reconstruction and Humanitarian Assistance began its work in Umm Qasr and subsequently moved to Baghdad. Several factors hampered its efforts. Jay Garner and later Paul Bremer were deployed with minimal resources according to a plan that had been devised only in January. Garner arrived with inadequate communications capability, and cooperation between his organization and Combined Land Forces Command initially faltered. Reconstruction got off to a slow start and did not provide adequate civilian services on the ground.

Particularly in the Sunni area, violence against U.S. forces, sabotage, and the truculence of local communities caused problems. Shi'ite leaders gave equivocal support at best. By July, the level of attacks in central Iraq indicated a full-fledged effort by Ba'athist hardliners, volunteers from outside Iraq, and possibly Ansar al-Islam and al-Qaeda operators to block U.S. reconstruction and inflict casualties that would affect U.S. commitment.

The question of whether the assigned forces were adequate to the original task reemerged; it will remain a subject for study by analysts and historians for some time. As a precursor to reconstruction, were there enough troops to accomplish the military objectives, then simultaneously disperse to Ba'athist seats of power and eliminate resistance? Back home in the United States, were high-level strategists overly optimistic about the Iraqi response to liberation and overconfident about the necessary link between the conventional military campaign and the peacekeeping efforts necessary to the development of democracy?

In retrospect, Iraqi Freedom was a tremendous military success. Several major developments stand out. General Tommy Franks and his leaders planned and fought a brilliant campaign that applied new technologies to traditional principles of military operation, achieving surprise and shock that shattered Iraqi will. Granted, the Iraqis fielded poorly trained forces and employed them in a hapless campaign plan. But Centcom's integration of service capabilities into a joint plan and its coordinated execution were truly extraordinary—perhaps only equaled in Operation Dragoon, the invasion of southern France in WWII, and Grant's capture of Vicksburg.

Iraqi Freedom confirmed an essential element of contemporary warfare: Air operations can provide a joint-force commander with firepower forward of the ground component's tactical zone. The campaign also highlighted the value of ground forces backed up by air support in outmaneuvering the enemy and striking quickly to disrupt his response. It demonstrated that the information technologies that allow distribution of battlefield information to every unit and headquarters—from the Pentagon's National Military Command Center to brigades, ships, and wings downrange—are a critical area for future defense planning and development. Additionally, Iraqi Freedom reinforced the importance of Special Operations Forces that can move stealthily to conduct raids and to direct precise strikes from the air and long-range artillery.

At least two issues require more extensive analysis. The tremendous logistics struggle in support of this campaign has received scant attention, and it was phenomenal in scope. Future investment in military capability should address the need to replace brute force logistics now used in modern warfare with ways of doing business enabled by information-age technologies. The second lesson, however, concerns our nation's ability to deploy forces as it did in the first phase of the operation. Without the long buildup and the wide deployment of assets before March 19, would the United States have been able to launch such a force quickly in a battle zone at strategic distance from homeland bases? The answer is no. Does the solution lie in lighter, reorganized ground-force units, fighter wings that require less strategic lift to move, or in more wide-body transport aircraft and fast sealift ships? What combination of these measures would be the most valuable in future campaigns?

The remaining strategic issue is more political than military. Currently, coalition forces are struggling with the unconventional tactics employed by Iraqi irregulars and Ba'athist remnants to undermine efforts to foster a new constituent government. These irregulars attack U.S. soldiers daily, and they have also attacked Iraqis who cooperated with the coalition. Additionally, jihadi fighters and terrorists have joined the conflict. We have taken

steps to form a new government in Iraq, but we have also created an unstable situation in the country. In the face of casualties and the halting progress of peacekeeping, will the United States have the discipline and national will to persist in this effort with all of its strategic consequences for the people of Iraq, their Arab neighbors, and the international community?

In Operation Iraqi Freedom, our troops performed magnificently. American strategy, operational art, applied technology, and combat leadership defeated the Iraqis just as they did the Taliban in Afghanistan. Information-age technologies produced an integration of service capabilities and national agencies to support the most disciplined joint campaign ever conducted. Operation Iraqi Freedom demonstrated that the U.S. military is exploiting transformational information technologies and that the combatant commanders are improving the art of joint operations. Perhaps the fervent call for transformation of the U.S. military is less urgent than continuing to advance the art of joint operations and finding more effective ways of dealing with the sources of conflict, terror, and the proliferation of weapons of mass destruction.

FIRST STRIKE

Throughout the day of March 19, 2003, the Pentagon guidance had been "Tonight is not the night." So the time and the way the war began came as a surprise to NBC News, the rest of the media, and even many of the armed forces who were to wage it. "Shock and awe," after all, had been the operative phrase—a massive air strike designed to induce those twin responses in the Iraqi leadership and military establishment.

It was supposed to be sustained and overwhelming, aimed at strategic targets throughout Baghdad. It didn't happen that way.

President George W. Bush addresses the nation from the Oval Office, March 19. *Left:* An Air Force KC-135 tanker from the 100th Air Refueling Wing, stationed in England, refuels one of four F-15C Eagles on their way to escort U.S. bombers. No air strikes could be mounted on targets in Iraq without the aid of the flying gas stations.

1

Below: President George W. Bush addresses the nation from the Oval Office, March 19. *Right:* One of forty Navy Tomahawk sea-launched cruise missiles leaves the deck of the guided missile cruiser USS *Bunker Hill* on March 20 Baghdad time to strike Doura Farms, reported by intelligence sources as being used by Saddam Hussein and his sons.

Instead, President Bush went on television and used a different phrase to announce the start of the war. He said strikes had been launched against "targets of military opportunity." That "opportunity" transformed the evening of March 19.

At NBC News headquarters in New York, executive producer Mark Lukasiewicz had put control room 3A on full alert at 5 A.M. Like all control rooms, 3A is a paradoxical place. Sealed off from the world—no windows, no natural light, no fresh air—it sees more than any other place can. There are over 150 TV monitors in 3A. At any one time, some forty different video feeds would be on display

Executive producers man the NBC control room in New York. Mark Lukasiewicz deploys the NBC troops, while Steve Capus and Beth O'Connell keep abreast of the images and reports flowing in from around the world.

throughout the war. Executive producer Steve Capus, who tracked many of them, notes, "The control room is the nerve center for live TV production. Its very design is centered on the concept of bombardment. Five dozen monitors hanging from the wall and even the ceiling bombard you with images."

That evening, NBC News executives and producers were watching those screens intently. News president Neal Shapiro was among them, and he recalls, "I scanned the monitors looking for any sign of explosions or anti-aircraft fire, but I always kept one eye on Mik."

"Mik" is Jim Miklaszewski, NBC's correspondent at the Pentagon, where all day the message had been "Not today . . . no action today."

It was the same message at Central Command headquarters in Doha, Qatar.

Correspondent Kelly O'Donnell remembers that "body language, blank faces, and talk of getting a good night's sleep" suggested that this was not the night the attack would come.

Something was odd, however. The White House, which usually issues a "full lid" signaling an end to the day's news, had instead issued only a "photo lid." NBC White House correspondent Campbell Brown was keeping a close watch on the West Wing offices, and she sent urgent messages to New York saying that no one had left yet. Then, for the first time in anyone's memory, the White House pressroom was "un-lidded."

Just after 9:30 P.M. eastern time, sirens blared in Baghdad. Mik said, "It's beginning. I'm sure."

Shapiro said, "Let's go."

Capus to Tom Brokaw in the studio: "Mik's got it. We're going."

Control room 3A (two voices at once): "Air-raid sirens! Air-raid sirens!"

Director: "Break us in! Break us in! We're on the air!"

Announcer: "This is an NBC News Special Report. Target Iraq."

Immediately, Brokaw called on Peter Arnett, who was reporting for *National Geographic* and NBC News from Baghdad. The scene there was confusing; it hardly conjured up the image of "shock and awe." Arnett reported, "There are sirens sounding all over Baghdad as of this moment. It's about an hour before dawn. Sirens sounding but no sound of missiles or anti-aircraft fire. No sign of any attack." Moments later: "Tom, the sound of several planes flying over the city and what seemed to be explosions in the outskirts of Baghdad. To the north, we're hearing anti-aircraft fire."

From the Pentagon, Miklaszewski reported, "Lasting only ten minutes, dozens of American bombs and missiles rained down on only a handful of Iraqi leadership targets. Not exactly the kind of devastating bombing first planned in the Pentagon's campaign of shock and awe. Instead, it's very tightly focused on driving out Saddam Hussein."

NBC's military analysts were taken aback both by what had happened and what had not. The attack was not massive, and it came near dawn instead of deep in the night. Retired General Barry

Below: Baghdad awoke at 5:30 A.M. to air-raid sirens, anti-aircraft fire, and finally explosions as Doura Farms was attacked. *Bottom:* These satellite photos show the wooded residential compound, before the bombing, *bottom left,* and after, *bottom right.*

McCaffrey, now an NBC military analyst, thought it was highly unusual. "They will absolutely have stunned the Iraqis," he told Brokaw. "Not a one of them would assume this would happen just prior to dawn. Overwhelming surprise." He added, "You know, I'm actually in shock and awe myself."

What happened was this: Four U.S. surface ships and two attack submarines fired forty Tomahawk cruise missiles, and two F-117 Nighthawk stealth fighter aircraft each dropped two laser guided bombs on a leadership compound in eastern Baghdad. The U.S. was acting on intelligence from a CIA source that senior members of the Iraqi regime, including Saddam Hussein and one or both of his sons, were inside the compound.

The information had reached CIA Director George Tenet about eight hours earlier. At 2 P.M., Tenet brought the information to Defense Secretary Donald Rumsfeld, and an hour later they brought it to the White House. A four-hour meeting ensued. At 7 P.M., the president ordered the strike.

Top: One of two F-117 Nighthawk stealth fighters lands in Qatar on March 20 after bombing Doura Farms. *Above:* NBC News anchor Tom Brokaw delivers special coverage of the unfolding surprise attack.

5

BY AIR AND SEA

A GIANT MACHINE. *Previous page:* On board the aircraft carrier USS *Harry S Truman.* Each section assigned to work on the carrier flight deck wears a distinctive color shirt: purple shirts or "grapes" are fuelers; green shirts man the catapults and arresting gear; red are the ordnance crew; blue shirts move planes around the deck; yellow are the traffic cops. *Clockwise:* Air Force munitions specialists load an air-launched cruise missile on a B-52 heavy bomber. The Louisiana-based bombers deployed to Guam in the Pacific Ocean and were kept at the ready to bomb on the first full night of operations. An F-14D Tomcat from the "Black Lions" of Fighter Squadron Two Thirteen and an F/A-18 Hornet from the "War Party" of Strike Fighter Squadron Eighty Seven move into launch position on board the USS *Carl Vinson* in the Mediterranean Sea, March 20. Rows of satellite-guided two-thousand-pound Joint Direct Attack Munitions (JDAMs) are transported to the flight deck by one of four elevators on board the USS *Harry S Truman.* Pilots assigned to Carrier Air Wing Two on board the USS *Constellation* listen to a preflight brief in their squadron ready room. ▦

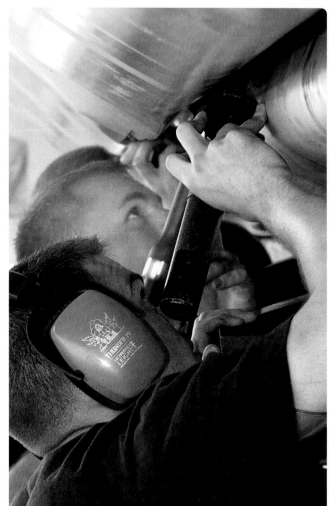

Above: An S-3B Viking surveillance aircraft launches from one of four steam-powered catapults aboard USS *Kitty Hawk* in the Persian Gulf, March 20. *Right:* A radar navigator runs a weapons targeting check during a B-52 bombing mission. *Opposite top:* The Combined Air Operations Center (CAOC) at Prince Sultan Air Base, Saudi Arabia, buzzes with activity. Lieutenant General T. Michael "Buzz" Moseley, the coalition air commander, controlled all aircraft and long-range strike missions from the supermodern facility, fifty miles south of Riyadh. *Opposite bottom:* President Bush meets with his national security and communications advisers after authorizing military operations on March 19. *Pictured left to right:* Steve Hadley, deputy national security adviser; Karen Hughes, special adviser to the president; General Richard Myers, chairman of the Joint Chiefs of Staff; Dan Bartlett, communications director; Vice President Dick Cheney; President Bush; Donald Rumsfeld, secretary of defense; Condoleezza Rice, national security adviser; and Secretary of State Colin Powell.

At the Pentagon, few knew of these developments. The building was emptying out, and Miklaszewski was preparing to leave. He made one last call to check on an unrelated story, a report that a terrorist suspect had been arrested overseas.

Miklaszewski later remembered that during the conversation, the official said to him, "By the way, do you know the president's going to address the nation tonight?"

Miklaszewski asked, "Is the war starting?"

The source replied, "Why else?"

In his television address, President Bush said, "These are the opening stages of what will be a broad and concerted campaign."

On NBC, Tom Brokaw said, "The war is effectively under way."

11

COUNTDOWN

SAND TABLE. *Right:* Soldiers of the 3rd ID wait out a chemical alert along the Iraqi border inside their Bradley Fighting Vehicle. *Next page spread, clockwise from top left:* A 3rd ID pep rally near the southern Iraqi border. Marines get their final war briefing of the eastern attack on Baghdad with old-fashioned paper maps and a sand table. 1st Division Marines some thirteen miles south of the Iraqi border know their way home is through Baghdad. Marines with Task Force Tarawa, 2nd Marine Expeditionary Brigade, try on their chemical-protection suits. *Following page spread:* Soldiers of the 101st Airborne Assault Division cram into a concrete bunker during a Scud missile alert in Kuwait. ▨

CHAPTER 2

BEFORE THE BEGINNING

Planning for news coverage of the war had been in the works for months, with an extra incentive to think imaginatively about how to report this war. A new phrase was about to enter the national vocabulary: "embedded reporters."

In all, there were to be more than six hundred journalists embedded with U.S. and British forces. For NBC News, there would be four teams led by correspondents:

David Bloom—3rd Battalion, 15th Infantry of the 2nd Brigade, 3rd Infantry Division (Mechanized)

Kerry Sanders—2nd Battalion, 8th Marines of Task Force Tarawa (2nd Marine Expeditionary Brigade)

Chip Reid—3rd Battalion, 5th Marines of the 1st Marine Division

Dana Lewis—2nd Brigade, 101st Airborne Division (Air Assault)

Bloom, convinced that war was a near certainty, had been pondering the possibilities since the previous year. He was thirty-nine, a former White House correspondent, and cohost of *Weekend Today*.

Far left: NBC correspondent David Bloom jots down notes on March 18 after hearing President Bush's ultimatum to Saddam Hussein, giving him and his two sons forty-eight hours to leave Iraq or face the consequences. *Left:* Embedded journalists receive gas-mask training in Kuwait City two weeks before the war. More than six hundred journalists initially embedded with military units, a number that would increase by two hundred as so-called unilaterals hooked up with amenable commanders.

Above: One half of the "Bloommobile" was actually an M88A tank recovery vehicle with a mounted gyro-stabilized camera. *Right:* The other half, a Ford F-450 extended cab truck, contained the satellite uplink and technical equipment. David Bloom was accompanied by Craig White, Paul Nassar, Bob Lapp, Jacob Kooser, and Bernie Plunkett.

But now he was determined to be on the leading edge of the action. On the afternoon of New Year's Eve, Bloom e-mailed his boss.

"I keep coming back to this idea: would it be possible to cover the battle-field live, from the onset of a ground war—so that the American people could actually watch that first line of troops crossing into Iraq, and then follow them—live—as they make their way toward Baghdad?

"I think the answer is yes."

Bloom's idea was right; hundreds of thousands of dollars later, it would come to pass. The plan called for the use of a broadcast-quality camera instead of a "videophone," which permits live transmission from anywhere but whose picture quality is far inferior to a camera's. That notion, in turn, gave birth to what came to be called the "Bloommobile."

It actually was two vehicles. Bloom and his cameraman, Craig White, rode atop a tank recovery vehicle, an M88A. A gyro-stabilizing platform enabled the camera to take steady pictures while the M88A roared through the desert. The signal was microwaved back several miles to a satellite uplink that engineer Bob Lapp called "Tina." That dish was attached to a truck that Lapp called "Ike" and that White described as a "stealth" vehicle: "The Bloommobile was a strange concept. We were lucky to get it because it was the high-tech part that beamed the picture back to the United States by satellite."

Lucky, perhaps.

But there was another factor in play.

Bloom had argued repeatedly with Pentagon officials who wanted to limit the number of nonmilitary vehicles in Iraq. He turned to

retired General Barry McCaffrey, arguing that banning the vehicle "makes no sense and undercuts the reasons for permitting the embeds in the first place."

What reasons?

"The Pentagon," Bloom wrote, "wants its soldiers' stories told honestly and objectively." In pleading his case, Bloom also highlighted

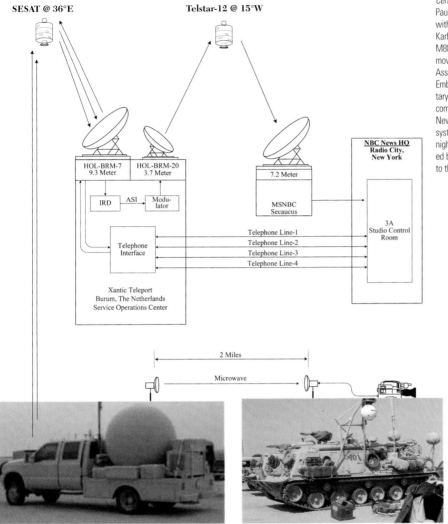

The Bloommobile System

SESAT @ 36°E

Telstar-12 @ 15°W

HOL-BRM-7
9.3 Meter

HOL-BRM-20
3.7 Meter

7.2 Meter

NBC News HQ
Radio City,
New York

IRD — ASI — Modulator

MSNBC
Secaucus

3A
Studio Control
Room

Telephone Line-1
Telephone Line-2
Telephone Line-3
Telephone Line-4

Telephone
Interface

Xantic Teleport
Burum, The Netherlands
Service Operations Center

2 Miles

Microwave

The Bloommobile in action. *Previous page, top:* Interior of the Bloommobile equipment racks. *Center:* Bloom with Craig White, Bob Lapp, and Paul Nassar broadcasting a live shot on March 27 with the 3rd Battalion, 15th Infantry, south of Karbala. *Bottom left:* David Bloom on board his M88A, broadcasting on the move as the 3rd ID moved rapidly through the Iraqi desert to Tactical Assembly Area Spartan 4. *Bottom right:* Embedded reporters ate and slept with their military units. *Left:* A schematic of the Bloommobile's complex communications path to New York and New Jersey. The M88A Wescam robotic camera system included stabilized pan/tilt/zoom with night vision capability. The camera was connected by a three-to-five-mile-range microwave link to the satellite uplink.

the obvious: The embedding process was not merely a concession to the media. It was meant to serve the Pentagon's purposes as well.

Looking back on that formative stage, Bloom's producer, Paul Nassar, observed that the whole point was to "democratize our coverage of the war."

Craig White, referring to the Gulf War twelve years earlier, noted, "If you ask anyone who they remember, they mention Colin Powell and Norman Schwarzkopf and no one else. We wanted to

Above: NBC producer Paul Nassar in an Army Bradley Fighting Vehicle. *Right:* Craig White eats an MRE while sitting on the M88A Bloommobile "blade."

change that. This was going to be a view of war through the eyes of common soldiers."

In the end, the Bloommobile was quietly flown to Kuwait where it was painted sand color and kept under wraps. Not until the war was under way, and Bloom was broadcasting high-quality television pictures while speeding through southern Iraq with the 3rd ID, did it become clear what the Bloommobile really was.

Kerry Sanders, from NBC's Miami bureau, had a different challenge. At forty-two, he already had considerable combat coverage

24

Clockwise from above left: NBC correspondent Kerry Sanders. Sanders reporting from the battlefield with the 2nd Battalion, 8th Marines, after crossing the Iraqi border. Sebastian Rich, Kerry Sanders's cameraman. Journalists, *left to right,* James Mates of British ITN; Danny Miller, NBC engineer; Sebastian Rich, NBC cameraman; Kerry Sanders.

experience, including Kosovo and Afghanistan. Now he had a problem. He was not embedded, his travels were not sanctioned by the Pentagon, and NBC planned that he would be what is termed a unilateral reporter. That usually means going where you choose and covering what you want, and journalists tend to welcome that freedom. But now Sanders was wary.

"Unilateral usually means on your own. In this case, I figured it would mean 'go nowhere.'"

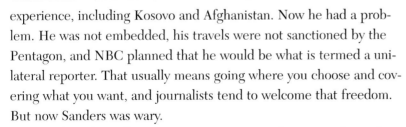

He reached out to a Marine Corps commander who, acting unilaterally himself, instantly invited Sanders to join the so-called 2/8.

The officer did not clear the invitation with the Department of Defense because, as Sanders recalls, "We agreed it would be highly unlikely that someone at the DoD would consult a list and ask, 'Why is Kerry Sanders there? He's not on the official embed list.'" The assumption was correct; nobody ever questioned Sanders's presence as an embed with the 2/8.

Dana Lewis also found a cooperative military officer. A Moscow-based correspondent, the forty-four-year-old Lewis had seen extensive

Top: NBC correspondent Dana Lewis with an officer of the 101st Airborne Division. Lewis was accompanied by Lai Ling Jew, Bill Angelucci, and Sam Sambataro. Much of the 101st would spend a good portion of the war fighting Fedayeen militia in the Shi'ite city of Najaf. *Above:* Dana Lewis reporting live during a missile alert in Kuwait with his gas mask on. *Right:* Reporting from the Kufa Soda Factory ("Kufa Cola"), outside Najaf in southern Iraq.

battlefield action in the Middle East, Somalia, Chechnya, Kosovo, and Afghanistan. Now he, too, had a problem: Only two places, for a correspondent and a cameraman, had been assigned to NBC in the 101st Airborne.

Two more were needed—a producer and an engineer to operate a satellite dish, making live transmission possible. Lewis's sympathetic officer "overlooked" Pentagon public affairs guidance and allowed a total of four places, confirming the correspondent's long-held conviction: "Incredibly, the public affairs officer was frustrated that NBC was granted those extra spots. It's my experience that the army's public affairs officers are trained to stop reporters from reporting. So my rule is—always talk to the commanders who are thirsty to have their units documented. Dodge the PAOs."

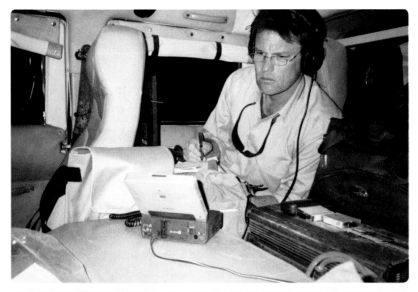

Chip Reid, a Burbank-based correspondent, had his own obstacle to overcome. At forty-eight, he was the oldest of NBC's embedded reporters, yet he was the only one without wartime experience, and no one in his family had a military background. A drastic learning curve was mandatory, so Reid made lists.

Reid did not know if he would be on the front lines or back with the supply lines. "I wanted to be up front," he recalls, "but with no military experience, I didn't know exactly what that meant." He found out soon enough: "My first meeting with the officers of my battalion

Top left: NBC correspondent Chip Reid, in his Humvee with video editing equipment. Reid's team included John Zito, Joe Klimovitz, and Rob Grant. *Top right:* A page out of Reid's notebook, with his crib sheet of the ranks of enlisted Marines and officers of his unit, the 3rd Battalion, 5th Marines. *Below left:* Set up at a Marine encampment in southern Iraq. *Above:* Chip Reid.

Soldiers were able to talk to their families on NBC satellite phones, in southern Iraq, March 28.

was a real jaw-dropper. I could be as far up front as I wanted. They stressed the danger. So I was going to get the kind of front line access I wanted, but I'd be lying if I said I wasn't scared."

The NBC teams were soon embedded with their respective units, and the question became, "Would they fit in?"

Phones broke the ice. At the 101st Airborne, NBC engineer Sam Sambataro connected a half dozen telephones to his satellite dish. Word spread that the phones were available and free, and soon there were long lines of soldiers anxious to call home and catch up on family news. Sambataro remembers one soldier who did not know what to do about his upcoming anniversary: "I gave him a step-by-step process—notes, flowers—and on the Internet we found a florist near his home-town. And when he got off the phone later that night he came back with the biggest smile and the biggest 'thank you' because his wife was just overjoyed with the roses. We made him spend fifty bucks,

28

too, 'cause he probably would have only spent ten."

Other NBC embedded units soon adopted the free phones practice. One NBC engineer, Bob Lapp, did not fully appreciate the value of the telephone gambit until well into the war: "If I could give one piece of advice to any future embeds, it would be to make close friends with the first and master sergeants. These guys run the army and can get you anything! We had helped out a couple of first sergeants early in the war with phone calls to their families, and now we were golden. All we had to do was mention something we needed and BAM! We had it.

"I think these guys understood that as long as we were down, there'd be no phones, so let's get this thing up and running, pronto!"

Producer Lai Ling Jew was NBC News's only female embedded journal-ist going into Iraq. She had heard what she called "rumblings of concern" that soldiers might endanger themselves to protect her. To her relief, it never happened, and the gender issue arose only in one playful incident.

An officer set up a shelf to divide her sleeping space from the fifteen soldiers in the tent they shared. That seemed to solve the privacy issue, until she learned that some of the men were field-testing their night-vision goggles inside the tent.

"From that moment forward," she joked, "I learned to change inside my sleeping bag. I'm pretty fast now."

Back in New York, the final preparations were falling into place. Collaborating with an environmental group, the Natural Resources Defense Council, producer Bob Windrem assembled a database of

Top: Producer Lai Ling Jew, NBC's only female embedded journalist, with the 101st Airborne in Kifl between Najaf and Hillah. *Above:* NBC engineer Sam Sambataro connected a half dozen phones to his satellite dish to allow soldiers to call home.

29

NBC executive producer of special projects Mark Lukasiewicz, *lower left,* and executive director of specials planning Phil Alongi, *lower right,* control the action, while Bob Wright, GE vice chairman and NBC chairman/CEO, *upper left,* and NBC News president Neal Shapiro, *upper right,* look on.

satellite photos, maps of most Iraqi cities, weather satellite images, and geological data.

In computer terms, NBC had access to more than 125 gigabytes—equivalent to the capacity of about six laptops—of data from NRDC alone. That was augmented in the coming days by photos taken by the Associated Press, Reuters, and Agence France-Presse. Technical plans, the most elaborate ever undertaken by NBC News, were completed.

Executive producer Mark Lukasiewicz, who had been coordinating the planning for two months, issued NBC's broadcast plan. He noted, "This is a massive undertaking. It will involve long hours and hard work. But it is hard to imagine a more important story."

One sentence in the memo was underlined and stated, "Please remember that the safety and security of our many colleagues in the war zone is our highest priority."

All was ready. The embeds had gone through a weeklong course called Hostile Environment Training as well as training at Defense

Department schools. They had signed documents that were reminders, if any were needed, of what might lie ahead.

"Release, Indemnification, and Hold Harmless Agreement and Agreement Not to Sue."

"The embedding process will expose media employees to all hazards of a military environment, including but not limited to the extreme and unpredictable hazards of war."

"Anthrax Vaccine Series"

"Smallpox Vaccine"

"Protective Mask Quantitative Fit-Test Program"

The U.S. military, fond of phrases, called the 3rd ID "the tip of the spear," the leading edge of the campaign. Bloom, Sanders, Lewis, and Reid—along with their producers, cameramen, and technicians—were now the tip of NBC's spear.

And the spear was about to be launched.

Anchor Tom Brokaw prepares to go on the air from Studio 3C at 30 Rockefeller Plaza in New York.

31

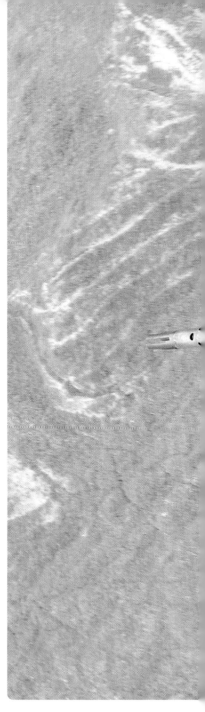

SPECIAL OPERATIONS

A NOT-SO-SECRET WAR. Task Force Viking, also known as Joint Special Operations Task Force North (JSOTF-N), was the most accessible of four separate Special Operations groups in Iraq; Task Force 20 was the most secretive. In mountainous northern Iraq, CIA paramilitary, covert operators, and military Special Operations had been operating for years before the war. *Next page:* Entire secret camps were set up to support the Kurdish and U.S. operation. Working in small teams with ultramodern equipment and transported by Air Force special operations helicopters, such as the MH-53 Pave Low, the shadow warriors could cover large areas, collecting intelligence, harassing Iraqi forces, attacking suspected terrorist hideouts, and supplying and directing Kurdish fighters. ▪

CHAPTER 3

SHOCK AND AWE

Almost immediately after the first air strikes, the rumors and reports began: Surrender talks have begun. Saddam is dead. Saddam is wounded; no, he's unscathed. His sons, Uday and Qusay, are wounded or dead; no, they survived. Is it really Saddam on TV? Why does he look tired and disoriented? When was his speech recorded?

Such questions were asked throughout the war; they were never satisfactorily answered. General Tommy Franks, commander of U.S. Central Command and the coalition's overall commander, was not preoccupied with these issues. He saw an opportunity and seized it, launching the invasion a day earlier than planned and before the true "shock and awe" bombing campaign began.

The 3rd ID swept across the Kuwait border. Its mission: Do not get bogged down on the way to Baghdad. The 3rd would conduct the fastest sustained military advance in history. David Bloom was part of

Far left: Smoke rises over Baghdad on March 22. Iraq ignited oil trench fires throughout the city in hope of complicating coalition reconnaissance and interfering with the guidance systems of U.S. weapons. Firdos circle, with the soon-to-be-famous statue of Saddam Hussein. *Above:* General Tommy Franks, the coalition commander, answers questions at a press conference in Doha, Qatar. *Left:* In Baghdad, an Iraqi watches Saddam Hussein speak on television soon after the initial bombing. The Iraqi leader's appearance would spark weeks of questioning: Where's Saddam?

The 3rd ID convoy passes through a former United Nations border-control checkpoint in the western Kuwaiti desert. The division would move 320 miles in only three days, the longest and fastest division move in history.

it. He reported, "We've been on the move in fits and starts for the last twenty-eight hours. We had three or four hours' sleep, but as these soldiers will tell you, the adrenaline tends to keep them pumped up."

On *Today*, Bloom invited Sergeant Joe Todd to send a message home: "Don't be worried, honey, everything's fine. We've got a lot of people out here to protect us and take care of us, and we're all taking care of each other."

The tip of the spear was now speeding through Iraq, but in truth the 3rd ID forces were not the first ones into the country. U.S., British, Australian, and Polish Special Operations Forces, along with CIA paramilitaries, already had infiltrated northern, western, and southern Iraq from Turkey, Jordan, Saudi Arabia, and Kuwait.

From the west, more than one thousand Special Operations troops attacked Iraqi airfields and command and control positions, sites from which surface-to-surface missiles could reach Israel. Because the forces had entered the country from Jordan and Saudi Arabia, the western front was especially sensitive and secret. No embedded journalists were assigned to these forces or, for that matter, to any other Special Operations Forces at any time during the war.

NBC got close. An Army Ranger regiment had invited NBC correspondent Tom Aspell to tag along, but Special Operations Command reversed that decision, and Aspell, a veteran of Middle East war reporting, watched the start of the war on television in a hotel room in Germany. Later, he was embedded briefly and uneventfully with an Air Force unit, but he spent most of the war as a unilateral reporter roaming northern Iraq.

NBC's Brian Williams got closer. He was anchoring in Kuwait for NBC and MSNBC, and that enabled him to see Special Operations units staging for missions into Iraq. Williams reported, "These are no

Left: A trio of heavily armed Navy SEAL patrol boats and a group of large inflatables await operations south of Kuwait City. *Above:* Tom Brokaw with Brian Williams, who anchored from his Kuwait base for the beginning of the war. Williams was accompanied by NBC analyst General Wayne Downing, retired, former commander of U.S. Special Operations Forces.

longer training runs. It's the real thing. These are the men of U.S. Special Operations, and they have never let a camera record these missions until now." As Williams pointed out, these men operated on something they called "the dark side."

"You'd hear it all over the place," he said. "'They've gone over to the dark side.' 'He's gonna go visit the dark side for a few days.' 'I knew you were on the dark side.' You hear it constantly."

And what happens on the dark side?

"It's one of the immutable truths of the dirty business of war that we have killers on our side," Williams observed. "And they are professional, trained killers."

Some Special Operations missions, however, were more about securing strategic facilities than targeting particular Iraqis. Along the Iraqi coast and near Basra, Navy SEALs and British Royal Marines, supported by other coalition Special Forces, raided oil terminals and facilities in the Persian Gulf, on the Faw peninsula, and the Rumaylah oil fields. The fields are Iraq's most productive: more than six hundred wells with a capacity to produce 1.3 million barrels a day. The goal was to gain control of those facilities before their defenders could put them to the torch. The Marines' mission was to secure those terminals and compounds, and the 3rd Battalion, 5th Marines headed that way.

Chip Reid remembers crossing the border. "It was a moonless night, with millions of stars. I could see the outline of the thirty-foot sand berm as we passed by; after that, nothing but the vague, flat whiteness of the desert." A tranquil image, perhaps, but it was shattered by the circumstances. Reid recalls, "It is the sound that I remember most clearly—the high-pitched, grinding roar of dozens of those steel behemoths filling the desert air with a noise that must have been terrifying to anyone in our path. That was my impression in the first moments of the war—loudly and violently hurtling through the darkness into Iraqi territory."

By the time Reid reached the oil and gas plants, several pipelines and nine oil wells were on fire. Coalition forces took control before any major explosions or destruction occurred, and for the most part, the southern oil facilities were saved. In the action around the Rumaylah fields, U.S. Marine Lance Corporal José Gutierrez was shot and killed, the first U.S. combat death of the war.

British coalition forces were on the move, too. Just hours before rolling across the border, Lieutenant Colonel Tim Collins, commander of the Royal Irish Battle Group, gave some final instructions to his troops. "If someone surrenders to you, then remember they have that right in international law. The ones who wish to fight—well, we aim to please. Our business now is north."

At the Pentagon, Secretary Rumsfeld made his first appearance of the war. He said that the assault to come would be unprecedented, "of

Previous page: 3rd ID armored vehicles push into southern Iraq at dusk. *Right:* The "steel rain" Multiple Launch Rocket System (MLRS) is capable of firing Army Tactical Missile System (ATACMS) guided missiles over 150 miles and shorter-range rockets almost twenty miles. The coalition ground advance followed not just air strikes on Iraqi forces, but artillery and MLRS strikes as well. *Below:* Secretary of Defense Donald Rumsfeld and Chairman of the Joint Chiefs of Staff Richard Myers regularly briefed reporters at the Pentagon on the progress of Operation Iraqi Freedom.

TORNADO FIGHTER IN FRIENDLY FIRE INCIDENT | MARINES BATTLE OUTSIDE NASIRIYAH | 3RD ID REACHES AREA WES

a force and a scope and a scale beyond what we have seen before."

Like the Special Operations war, the air campaign took place largely out of view. Reporters in Baghdad could see downtown being bombed, but in the northern towns of Mosul, Kirkuk, and Tikrit, and at hundreds of airfields, radar installations, missile batteries, and communications sites throughout the country, intense air strikes were out of camera range.

Something—three somethings, to be precise—flew in the opposite direction: Three Iraqi missiles were fired toward Kuwait. Two were intercepted by Patriot surface-to-air missiles, while the third landed near the headquarters of the 1st Marine Expeditionary Force. Then the lurking fear—the fear of chemical weapons—burst to the surface.

Alerts sounded throughout Kuwait. Dana Lewis was there with the 101st Airborne, and he recalls what it was like: "The fear. The

Top: A British AS90 Braveheart 155mm self-propelled artillery gun outside Basra, firing on Iraqi units and military installations. *Above:* Even after the initial coalition air strikes, soldiers in Kuwait endured numerous false alarms of chemical attack as they awaited their turn to enter Iraq.

43

Previous page: A Royal Marine from 42 Commando fires a Milan anti-tank wire-guided missile in southern Iraq. *Above:* The bat-winged B-2 bomber, which entered the fight on March 20. "On a single bombing sortie, a B-2 can hit sixteen separate targets, each with a 2,000-pound, precision-guided, satellite-based bomb," Vice President Dick Cheney said on April 9. *Right:* Air Force F-15Es are readied for bombing, March 21. The workhorse aircraft were part of the 379th Air Expeditionary Wing. The Wing's 180 combat aircraft dropped 3.2 million pounds of bombs. A single F-15E was lost in combat on April 7.

adrenaline. My decision not to go into the bunker but to go on the air. Frustrating. Feel angry and worn out by sirens. But always the fear it could be for real this time. You have nine seconds to get the gas mask and put it on."

Chip Reid recalls wearing just a T-shirt and gym shorts under his chemical suit. "Imagine a snow suit with a charcoal liner," he describes. "That's what it's like, and it can be extremely warm."

Sitting in the studio in New York, Tom Brokaw watched all this unfold. "I kept remembering all those pre-war briefings about the use

of chemical and biological weapons, and I dreaded the moment we'd have to report they had been launched. Thank God, they weren't."

The Iraqi missile offensive was a dud; throughout the war, not one Iraqi missile carried chemical weapons or resulted in death. They did cause some damage and civilian panic in Kuwait, but that was all.

"Shock and awe," however, was something else. On the third day of the war, aircraft from more than a dozen bases in the Gulf region, the United States, Europe, and the Indian and Pacific Oceans carried out almost one thousand strikes. More attacks came from five aircraft carriers, including the USS *Constellation*, where *Today*'s Ann Curry reported that the strike plan was fluid. "One pilot described it this way: 'It's like a street fight. You punch hard, then you step back, see what the situation is before you decide to punch again.'"

Hundreds of cruise missiles were fired at several hundred targets throughout Iraq, including Baghdad. From the high-rise Palestine Hotel, Peter Arnett described the scene: "Three major buildings, four, Tom, hit a mile away. . . . More explosions. . . . The blast hitting us in the room

Top: On March 21, more than twenty targets were attacked in the restricted government section of downtown Baghdad, including the offices of the Revolutionary Command Council, Iraq's highest-level ruling body. *Above: Today*'s Ann Curry reports from the aircraft carrier USS *Constellation*. During Operation Iraqi Freedom, *Constellation*'s aircraft flew more than 1,500 sorties and expended more than one million pounds of ordnance. Ships in the *Constellation* battle group fired 408 Tomahawk cruise missiles.

Saddam Hussein's offices, the Presidential Secretariat, and various offices and guard posts of the Special Security Organization charged with the Iraqi president's security were priority targets in downtown Baghdad. U.S. war planners hoped that the weakening of Saddam's normal personal security and transportation would open the way for a palace coup. The Council of Ministers, *background,* and Revolutionary Command Council, *foreground,* in downtown Baghdad burn after being bombed on March 21.

Above: Iraq's interior minister carries a chrome-plated Kalashnikov during an impromptu news conference on March 21. *Right:* Information Minister Mohammed Saeed al-Sahaf denounces Donald Rumsfeld as a "criminal dog" in one of his many appearances during the war.

here. . . . Violent explosions. . . . More. . . . More. . . . This is shock and awe, Tom, for the population of Baghdad. Shock and awe indeed."

(Peter Arnett reported for NBC News from Baghdad until March 30, when he was dismissed for giving an unauthorized interview to Iraqi television.)

Secretary Rumsfeld worried about how it looked on television: "The pictures made it look like we were bombing Baghdad. We were not bombing Baghdad. There are a large number of command and control and regime targets. And that is what we were bombing, and it

was very precise, and it made it look like the city was ablaze. The city was not ablaze. The Iraqi regime was ablaze."

Rumsfeld also dismissed comparisons between this air campaign and any that had gone before. "There is no comparison," he said. "The weapons that are being used today have a degree of precision that no one ever dreamt of in a prior conflict—they didn't exist."

Perhaps unintentionally, Iraq's Minister of Information, Mohammed Saeed al-Sahaf,

reinforced Rumsfeld's claim. He put the toll from the initial air strikes at 207 wounded. He did not mention any deaths, although the International Red Cross already had reported at least one civilian fatality during the first night's strikes. But as targets in Baghdad and elsewhere took a pounding, the Iraqi government's casualty count began to rise. "Shock and awe" set in. On March 24, for example, Iraq claimed that 252 civilians had been killed the day before, 194 of them in Baghdad.

The Iraqi regime also sought to reassure the nation about its leadership. Deputy Prime Minister Tariq Aziz appeared and claimed that Saddam and all his aides had survived and were in full control. On the same day, Saddam appeared twice on TV.

In the south, coalition ground forces were making quick headway. Elements of the 3rd ID attacked two air bases and blew past Nasiriyah, reaching the Euphrates River town of Samawah in three days.

To the east, British forces reached the edge of Basra, Iraq's second largest city, while British commandos completed an amphibious

Previous page, lower left: Marines prepare an AH-1 Cobra attack helicopter for operations in the south as, *above,* British forces decide on the next course of action outside Basra. The 7th Marine Regiment led the securing of the Rumaylah oilfields, while advance teams of Special Operations Forces attempted to block Iraq from sabotaging the infrastructure. Oil facilities were extensively booby-trapped, but only nine oil wells were successfully set ablaze.

Soldiers at Camp Pennsylvania in Kuwait carry a wounded comrade for medical treatment after a disgruntled fellow soldier allegedly tossed grenades into a command tent of the 101st Airborne Division. Two officers of the 1st Brigade were killed and fourteen were injured in the March 23 attack.

assault on the Faw peninsula. U.S. Marines attacked the Persian Gulf port town of Umm Qasr, through which humanitarian supplies would eventually flow.

Saddam's soldiers began to surrender. Three days into the conflict, there were more than 1,200 prisoners of war.

There were setbacks as well. A U.S. Marine Sea Knight helicopter crashed, killing four American and eight British troops. Two British Sea King helicopters collided, killing seven. A Patriot missile battery shot down a British Tornado fighter, leaving two dead. A suicide car bomb in Kurdish-controlled northern Iraq killed an Australian journalist. British and American forces fired on a British TV crew; one crew member died, and two remained missing long after the war was over.

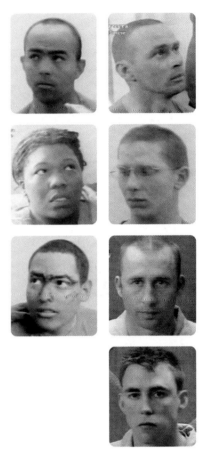

On March 23, at Camp Pennsylvania in Kuwait, a disgruntled U.S. soldier with the 101st Airborne allegedly tossed grenades and fired shots at his commanding officers, killing two.

On the same day, about fifty Apache helicopters, attacking far in front of the 3rd ID, came under heavy fire; thirty were damaged, one was downed, and two crewmen became the first U.S. prisoners of war.

Also on March 23, fighting erupted in Nasiriyah, and the 507th Maintenance Company got separated from the rest of the convoy it was traveling with, wound up on the wrong road, and ran into Iraqi forces. In all, thirteen men and two women were missing. The next day, five of them, along with the two captured Apache pilots, were shown on Iraqi TV. Bodies of some of the others were also shown. The United States objected and accused the Iraqis of violating the Geneva Conventions, but it would be many days before anyone learned the fate of these prisoners.

It would prove to be the worst day of the war for the coalition, even though Iraqi forces were being pummeled and coalition troops were advancing rapidly. If heavy fighting in Nasiriyah was a sign of what would happen in other populated areas, and if the Republican Guards entered the fight, it would be a battle indeed.

Now there was trouble. And there was about to be more.

Above left: Iraqi tribesmen, irregular fighters, and soldiers celebrate the downing of an Army AH-64 Apache attack helicopter east of Karbala. Amidst a massive sandstorm, Apache attack helicopters of Task Force 11th Aviation undertook a long-range mission against Republican Guard positions, receiving intense counterfire. Thirty helicopters were damaged and one was downed. Two captured pilots were later paraded on Iraqi TV on March 24. American POWs, *clockwise from top left,* Specialist Joseph Hudson, Sergeant James Riley, Private First Class Patrick Miller, Chief Warrant Officer David Williams, Chief Warrant Officer Ronald Young Jr., Specialist Edgar Hernandez, Specialist Shoshana Johnson.

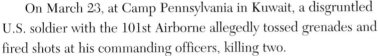

CHAPTER 4

STORM AND PAUSE

The trouble came from nature.

Chip Reid: "Imagine a sandstorm—sixty-mile-an-hour winds—in a world filled with orange baby powder. It was in your eyes, your ears, your nose, your throat."

Kerry Sanders: "It's like dust. You can't imagine something that small can hurt, but it hurts."

3rd Infantry Division soldier: "I wish we were home right now. I just can't wait to get back home."

Paul Nassar, producer for David Bloom, said it was unlike anything he had experienced: "It felt like we were plucked from Planet Earth and dumped on Jupiter. The sky would be clear one second, and then suddenly the sand would kick up, and the sky would

Far left: The 3rd Battalion, 69th Armor, 3rd Infantry Division, rolls through southern Iraq. As part of the 1st Brigade Combat Team, the battalion would establish a blocking position to isolate Najaf and then move on to south Baghdad before taking Saddam International Airport. *Left:* An Iraqi civilian struggles to navigate alongside U.S. troops in Nasiriyah as a furious sandstorm begins.

55

"We're in the midst of a vicious sandstorm in south central Iraq right now."

"Today has been a day of frustration for these soldiers. Sands whipping across the Iraqi desert all day, up to fifty miles an hour."

"I'm going to break another of these chem lights so you can get a little better view of us."

Above: Broad daylight and David Bloom requires light sticks for illumination while reporting in the sandstorm. *Right:* Bob Lapp and NBC satellite engineer Jake Kooser fix the antenna of the Bloommobile after the sandstorms clear.

become yellow and then orange and then crimson red. And from there, pitch black."

Engineer Bob Lapp, who operated and maintained the Bloommobile, recalls how difficult traveling was during the day, and how much worse at night: "And then the sun went down. I hate when that happens. As bad as the sand was during the day, for a rookie like me, following a tank at night was damn near impossible. Well, actually impossible, 'cause we got lost. Not 'I-can't-find-my-car-in-the-mall-parking-lot' lost. I mean, 'I-can't-find-my-seventy-ton-tank-in-a-hostile-country-during-a-sandstorm' type lost. Man, we were scared."

Cameraman Craig White had his own sand story, one that verged on the surreal. "I had a little cordless phone that connected me to New York," he said. "In the middle of this storm, my communications dropped out. Before I could hit redial, the phone rang. It was a telemarketer from Florida trying to sell me something. She thought I was in Florida. And I said, 'If you can deliver I might be interested.' Then I told her where I was, and she said, 'That's not nice; this is a serious war, you shouldn't joke about such things.' True story."

For the troops, it certainly was no joke. Chip Reid recalls that some were nervous at first because they could not see the enemy, but then they realized the Iraqis had the same problem. There also were the problems of sand getting into the machinery and wind breaking

31/03/2003

A soldier from the 3rd ID demonstrates the powerful winds of the sandstorm.

delicate equipment. It happened more than once to the Bloommobile, and that's when engineer Bob Lapp would turn to the soldier he called "Welder Guy."

"We all have had friends that were big talkers, not in the bragging sense but in the 'never shut the [expletive] up' sense. Dallas Diekman beats them all. Dallas was our welder friend and, in a way, the savior of the Bloommobile. This kid was a welding genius, and not only that, always willing and available to help us. The price was you had to listen to his stories. Oy."

The storms impeded, and sometimes stopped, the movement of various units, including Reid's Marine battalion, which was to head

SANDSTORM

ALMOST BIBLICAL. On March 24, even the most modern military units were humbled by a huge sandstorm. Day turned to night, winds reached 60 mph, and fine dust penetrated everything. Iraq is particularly susceptible to desert sandstorms because much of the country lies in a wind tunnel flanked by Turkish and Iranian mountain ranges, which force storm systems to curve down across the flat central and southern terrain into the Persian Gulf. The storm finally began to abate early on March 27, opening the way for helicopter operations for the first time in three days. ▪

through Nasiriyah and central Iraq before turning east toward the Tigris River and eventually assaulting southeastern Baghdad. The weather also delayed Bloom's 3rd Infantry Division brigade, which was to seize Euphrates River crossings before leading the attack on Saddam International Airport in western Baghdad, and Lewis's 101st Airborne brigade, poised to defeat the Fedayeen and Ba'ath Party militia in Najaf and Karbala, Iraq's two holiest Shi'ite cities. The storms also slowed down Sanders's Marine unit, the 2/8, which wound up spending eleven days in Nasiriyah.

Located on Highway 8 as it crosses the Euphrates River, Nasiriyah became the scene of some of the heaviest and most sustained fighting of the war. As Kerry Sanders put it, "The battle in Nasiriyah is not for control of this city. It's for ownership of Highway 8, which leads north toward Baghdad. Highway 8 is called by Marines 'Ambush Alley.'"

Left: A U.S. Marine runs for cover during an Iraqi mortar attack in southern Iraq. *Above:* Firdos circle in Baghdad, as seen from the Palestine Hotel. As sandstorms raged into southern Iraq, Baghdad also experienced its own bout of seemingly supernatural weather.

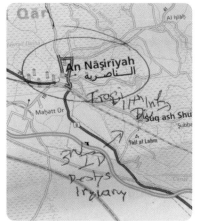

It was here that the irregular fighters known as "Fedayeen" emerged as a more potent force than Saddam's regular army. Instead of battling the Iraqi 11th Infantry Division, which largely dissolved, U.S. Marines faced men in civilian clothing who sniped from rooftops, schools, and mosques. Defense Secretary Donald Rumsfeld reported, "They dress in civilian clothes and operate from private homes confiscated from innocent people, and try to blend in with the civilian population. Their purpose is certainly not to make martyrs of themselves, but to make martyrs of innocent Iraqis opposed to Saddam's rule. But we will take them at their word, and if their wish is to die for Saddam Hussein, they will be accommodated."

The Iraqis fired rocket-propelled grenades and machine guns from pickup trucks, not tanks. There were some reports that Fedayeen waved a white flag of surrender, then opened fire. In the ensuing fight, nine Marines were killed and twenty were wounded. For the coalition, it was the war's most costly battle.

In the heat of urban warfare, there is increased risk of danger from friendly fire. It happened in Nasiriyah. Marines fired on what they thought were Fedayeen guerrillas. Four trucks were destroyed, and

Above: Nasiriyah would prove difficult to take and clear, but most of the combat was neither with Republican Guardsmen nor the Iraqi Army, but instead with Fedayeen fighters. Task Force Tarawa was given the job of making Highway 8 safe for supplies to move north. *Bottom right:* Marines search for friends missing after an intense firefight. *Opposite top:* Iraqi prisoners being held by 2nd Battalion, 8th Marines, in southern Iraq.

thirty-one men injured. NBC's Kerry Sanders described it as a mess: "Sunrise. Trucks are smoldering. Some of the men still walking around dazed. They can't believe that they had made it through this. Many of them very upset, furious to think they'd been fired on by their own people."

The Fedayeen attacks were not confined to Nasiriyah. Brian Williams, his producer Justin Balding, and NBC News consultant General Wayne Downing, retired, ended up on the receiving end of

Below: Kerry Sanders reports on the March 26 nighttime friendly fire incident involving the 2/8 Marines in Nasiriyah. A Marine artillery unit fired on 2nd Battalion positions over a ninety-minute period. Amazingly, no one was killed in the incident.

67

an ambush directed at the 3rd Infantry Division. An Army helicopter armada was delivering seventeen-thousand-pound sections of a pontoon bridge to Najaf, about one hundred miles south of Baghdad. The NBC team went along for the ride, occupying the third of four Chinook choppers.

As Williams later reported, "The Iraqi landscape looks quiet. Down below, some civilians, seemingly happy to see us." But General Downing, who had led Special Operations during the Gulf War and subsequently commanded all Special Operations Forces, was nervous. He saw pickup trucks—Nissans and Toyotas—with machine guns and other gear mounted on the back. Williams knew that Special Operations Forces were using such vehicles; he had seen them being loaded onto

Left: Seventeen incidents of friendly fire were investigated after Operation Iraqi Freedom. The worst known incident, according to the Center for Army Lessons Learned, occurred on March 23 when an Air Force A-10 attacked Marine Corps vehicles near Nasiriyah, killing nine Marines. *Above:* View from one of a group of CH-47 Chinook helicopters charged with delivering pontoon bridges north to the 3rd ID.

U.S. aircraft. But these were not Special Operations pickup trucks. Producer Justin Balding recalls, "One of the chopper crews ahead of us spotted a pickup truck. As the Iraqis waved, a man suddenly whipped off the tarpaulin to reveal another man armed with a rocket-propelled grenade launcher. He took aim and fired."

The grenade entered the helicopter's open tail, tore a hole in the fuselage, and grazed a crewman's face, but did not detonate. Williams pointed out, "There was some symbolism in all of this. A Vietnam-era RPG going clean through the tail of a Vietnam-era Chinook helicopter."

All four choppers landed quickly. Williams recalls General Downing saying, "We're in about the most dangerous place in the world right now, gentlemen." Almost immediately, however, they

With NBC anchor Brian Williams, producer Justin Balding, and analyst General Wayne Downing, retired, aboard, Army Chinook helicopters are forced to make a desert landing after being attacked by Iraqi Fedayeen. For two nights, the NBC crew and their Army unit waited out the fierce sandstorm in the desert.

were surrounded by 3rd Infantry Division forces. A soldier popped out of a Bradley armored vehicle and noticed that Downing was wearing a floppy hat that said "Class of '52." He saluted and said, "General, Lieutenant Eric Nye. West Point class of '99. What the hell are you doing here?"

The 3rd ID soldiers revealed that Fedayeen irregulars, not Republican Guard units, had been their sole adversaries in the war so far. Williams reported that it had "become a battlefield secret of sorts. These soldiers aren't quite fighting the war they expected to find here in Iraq."

Sandstorms grounded the NBC team in the desert for two nights.

But not everything was going wrong for coalition forces—far from it. Air strikes accelerated on Iraqi Republican Guard forces to the south of Baghdad. Attacks continued unabated on Saddam's regime in the capital. British forces moved closer to Basra in the south. U.S. and British Marines finally secured an important objective, the port town of Umm Qasr, opening the way for ships to deliver humanitarian

NBC analyst retired General Wayne Downing, *civilian clothes, left,* and NBC anchor Brian Williams, *civilian clothes, right,* confer with Lieutenant Erika Woods and Chief Warrant Officer Rich Krell.

aid. In the Kurdish-controlled area of Iraq, the 173rd Infantry Brigade arrived to help open a northern front, after Turkey refused permission for coalition forces to cross its territory.

The 3rd ID moved north so quickly that it was victimized by its own success. As the lines stretched out, it became harder to keep the 3rd supplied with fuel, ammunition, food, and water. David Bloom reported that storms shut down the convoy for four days: "Short on supplies and stalled in the desert, front line soldiers take up defensive positions as they wait for such basic necessities as food and water."

Even so, Captain Josh Wright of the 3rd ID insisted, "The mission will get done. It may not be as fast as everybody thinks or everybody wants, but this mission will get done. No doubt about it."

The storms, the ambushes—for Chip Reid it was "just chaos and confusion." Under attack one night, he remembers running first in one direction then another, trying to find safety. A Marine grabbed him and shoved him into a truck, where he found his engineer, Rob Grant. Reid called New York to report on the attack: "I told whoever

I was talking to in the control room that we were cowering in the back of a truck. Rob Grant said to me just before I went on the air, 'Chip, please don't tell them we're cowering. Just say that we have taken cover.'"

The harassment from the Fedayeen complicated the resupply effort, and the ferocious sandstorms would have made the resupply difficult with or without the ambushes.

Another storm was brewing back in the United States. Had the military misjudged the type of war the Iraqis would wage? Were there enough troops to protect the rear areas and also push forward toward Baghdad? Was there something wrong with the war plan?

Above: As the sandstorms ended, Ba'ath Party headquarters in nine locations were attacked by coalition air and ground forces. British forces moved to close northern routes into Basra as they secured the Basra refinery to the west of the city. *Next page:* A Marine carries his wounded comrade for medical aid in southern Iraq. Over six hundred coalition soldiers were wounded in fighting through mid-April.

CHAPTER 5

WAR OF WORDS

In a front-page article on March 25, the *Washington Post* stated,

> "With the Pentagon now rushing thousands of troops from Texas to the Persian Gulf, a number of seasoned Gulf War ground commanders said yesterday that the U.S. invasion force moving rapidly to Baghdad is too small and should have included at least one additional heavy Army division."

On *Today*, NBC analyst retired General Barry McCaffrey told Katie Couric, "We certainly didn't go up there with an overwhelming amount of strength. We're depending upon the most powerful air force in the world to make up for that lack of ground combat power."

The following day, the ranking Army officer in Iraq weighed in with his concerns. Lieutenant General William "Scott" Wallace, V Corps commander, was quoted as saying that overextended supply lines and Iraqi resistance had stalled the U.S. forward movement. He added, "The enemy we're fighting is different from the one we war-gamed against."

Left: A blindfolded Iraqi prisoner sings to himself outside an industrial complex in central Iraq. *Below:* General Tommy Franks denies reports that ground forces were ordered to halt their advance on Baghdad because of resistance. For five days, Franks and other U.S. leaders fielded questions about the pace of the war and the soundness of the war plan.

77

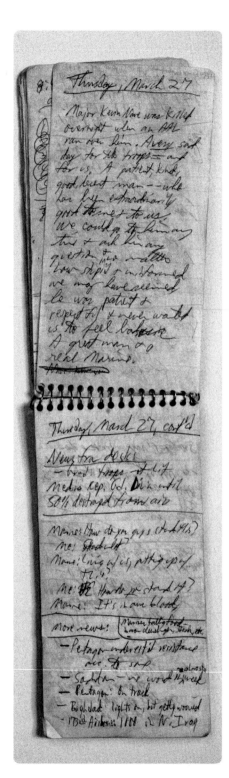

That evening, Tom Brokaw reported, "At the moment, things are not going exactly as U.S. military planners had hoped. They were able to move their armored and Marine units very swiftly north. But falling in behind them were irregular forces still loyal to Saddam Hussein, and they can interrupt the supply flow."

Another NBC military analyst, retired General Montgomery Meigs, told Katie Couric, "We've seen that the Iraqis have generated some capabilities that are, perhaps, more robust than we thought."

VETERANS QUESTION WAR STRATEGY
Guardian (London), March 26

FORMER COMMANDERS QUESTION U.S. STRATEGY
Los Angeles Times, March 26

U.S. IN COMBAT UNDER CONSTRAINTS
USA Today, March 26

WAR COULD LAST MONTHS, OFFICERS SAY
Washington Post, March 27

TACTICAL ANALYSTS FEEL NO AWE
Australian, March 27

RUMSFELD FAULTED FOR TROOP DILUTION
Washington Post, March 30

CRITICS: U.S. TOOK GUERRILLAS LIGHTLY
Chicago Tribune, March 30

The Pentagon fired back, first mildly and then strongly. "No plan, no matter how perfect, survives first contact with the enemy," said General Richard Myers, chairman of the Joint Chiefs of Staff.

Defense Secretary Rumsfeld said the coalition had made "solid progress" in the first week of the war: "We have seen mood swings in the media from highs to lows to highs and back again, sometimes in a single twenty-four-hour period. For some, the massive TV, the massive volume of television—and it is massive—and the breathless reports can seem to be somewhat disorienting."

Now that the talk of a prolonged campaign had become so widespread, President Bush, who was meeting with British Prime

NEW YORK   WASHINGTON, DC

TARGET: IRAQ

Above: NBC *Today* anchor Katie Couric interviews NBC analyst General Barry McCaffrey, retired, on March 25. "In my judgment, there should have been a minimum of two heavy divisions and an armored cavalry regiment on the ground," McCaffrey had told the *Washington Post. Far left:* An excerpt from Chip Reid's notebook.

Minister Tony Blair at Camp David, was asked just how long it would be. "However long it takes," he said. "That's the answer to your question, and that's what you've got to know. It's not a matter of timetables. It's a matter of victory." On April 1, General Myers bluntly complained about the ongoing debate: "It is not helpful to have those kind of comments come out when we've got troops in combat because they're false, they're absolutely wrong, they bear no resemblance to the truth, and it's just harmful to our troops that are out there fighting very bravely, very courageously."

An NBC military analyst remembers that he and his colleagues at NBC and elsewhere all reacted to Myers's comment in the same way: Since the troops in Iraq were hardly tuning in to television and radio every day to follow the debate, the retired officers felt sure Myers was sending a message directly to them.

Later in the war, as Baghdad was falling and the regime was disappearing, Vice President Dick Cheney was still talking about the war of words that had since died down. The actual war, he said, had "proceeded according to a carefully drawn plan with fixed objectives and

flexibility in meeting them. In the early days of the war, the plan was criticized by some retired military officers embedded in TV studios."

There were conflicting messages and clashing assessments everywhere. NBC News vice president Bill Wheatley passed a newsstand where a pair of headlines caught his eye. In *USA Today*: ALLIES COUNT DAY OF SUCCESSES. In *Newsday*: BOGGED DOWN.

Wheatley e-mailed everyone at NBC News: "A week into the war in Iraq, the only thing that seems clear is that it's *not* clear how well the war is going. Opinions on that vary widely, even within the military. For us, this makes it a time for caution."

It certainly was that for executive producer Steve Capus, who spent a large part of every day in control room 3A confronted by a remarkable array of possibilities. "What struck me over and over again," Capus observed, "was just how difficult it was to bring the big

Opposite top left: President Bush and Secretary of Defense Rumsfeld leave the Pentagon's National Military Command Center where they received the latest war briefings on March 25. Bush visited the Pentagon to announce his $74.7 billion wartime supplemental budget request, appearing with, *opposite bottom:* Rumsfeld and Deputy Secretary of Defense Paul Wolfowitz. *Left:* NBC anchor Tom Brokaw, *center,* sits in Studio 3C with NBC's retired military cadre: *left to right,* Lieutenant General Michael Short, USAF, retired, who commanded the NATO air campaign in Yugoslavia in 1999; General Montgomery Meigs USA, retired, former commander of U.S. Army Europe; General Barry McCaffrey, USA, retired, commander of the 24th Infantry Division (Mechanized) in the first Gulf War; and Vice Admiral Dennis McGinn, USN, retired, former commander of the 3rd Fleet and deputy chief of naval operations.

picture into focus. The images coming back from the battlefield were often startling, but what did those pictures really tell us about the overall war effort?"

The same question nagged at the embedded journalists.

Producer Lai Ling Jew commented, "It was strange. I was in a news blackout even though I was covering the biggest story. We were in the middle of it, but all we were getting was one view of everything. We knew that, and we always wanted the full pie. It was a strange feeling for a journalist to only have this little slice."

Of course, the embedded journalists were far away, shielded from the debate raging back home. But Capus and his colleagues in New York and Washington were not shielded. They were in the thick of it, besieged by opinions from everywhere. Capus notes, "America is wired for instant reaction. The e-mails came in by the hundreds from people who thought we were being unfair and even unpatriotic for airing criticism of the war plan. Still others thought we weren't being tough enough on the military brass. Who was right?"

As Capus pointed out, the same standard had to be applied to U.S. briefings and Iraqi government statements since "it stands to reason that public officials are going to try to present their views in the best possible light."

In Doha, Qatar, for example, NBC's Kelly O'Donnell described to Matt Lauer the press corps' growing frustration with the content of

Next page: A cemetery in southern Iraq. Fighting raged near schools, mosques, cemeteries, and hospitals, all of which were used by Iraqi forces for cover.

Top: Protesters gather in front of the White House as war commences. *Above: Today* anchor Matt Lauer and correspondent Kelly O'Donnell, both reporting from Centcom headquarters in Qatar.

the military briefings at the high-tech $250,000 Centcom headquarters. "There has been a lot of repetitive information in the briefings," O'Donnell said. "There's been a lot of restating the administration's message about wanting to liberate the Iraqi people. Repeatedly today, General Vincent Brooks said, 'This is a podium for truth.' He said it over and over and over again. That is about message, not about information for those of us trying to file stories."

Different messages were coming from different places. NBC correspondent Dawna Friesen was in Cairo monitoring the war that the Arab world was seeing, and she reported: "If Americans and Arabs have one thing in common right now, it's that they're riveted to their televisions—in many cases seeing the same pictures, but looking at

Left: An Iraqi bus sits immobilized after being bombed in western Iraq. The Amman-Baghdad highway became a crater-pocked route as coalition air attacks sought to isolate the capital and impede movement in the western desert. *Below:* Army war planners and logisticians track the status of ground forces and funnel information to senior commanders for decisions.

85

Top: During a press conference in Baghdad, Iraqi military authorities provided their own update of the military situation. Above: Dateline NBC correspondent Mike Taibbi reporting from Amman, Jordan.

them from very different perspectives. On Egypt TV, the evening news headline was about five Iraqis killed in the bombing of Baghdad. Iraqi casualties are mentioned and shown far more frequently than on U.S. TV."

Correspondent Mike Taibbi experienced this dichotomy first-hand. He spent much of the war in Ruwayshid, Jordan, near the Iraqi border, with Arab colleagues and staff. In one room of the NBC office, Taibbi kept the TV tuned to NBC or MSNBC. In another room fourteen steps away, the Arab men watched Arab TV, principally al-Jazeera. Taibbi recalls, "At noon, the lead story in our room was the supposed four-to-six day pause in the infantry's advance toward Baghdad. But the lead story in Ghazi's room was another bombing in another Baghdad marketplace with graphic video of the dead and another claim that civilians were targeted deliberately."

Taibbi noted that they all—Americans and Arabs—got along, sharing meals, playing sports. But, he added, "We are being urged, by the stories we're seeing, to different conclusions about why men in the desert next door are killing each other. The things that connect us, connect us less every day."

Back in the United States, the clashing impressions continued. On CNBC, Forrest Sawyer called it "a strangely schizophrenic perception of this war." He continued, "Some are saying the original plan was misguided, not enough force on the ground and overconfident assessment of the enemy. Others say the war is right on track, remarkable gains have been made in such a short time, and there is way too much hand-wringing going on."

Even after the pause ended, Rumsfeld pressed his case. "We're within forty-nine miles of Baghdad," he said. "There are so many

President Bush is briefed by Dan Morris, Centcom assistant director of intelligence, at MacDill Air Force Base in Tampa, Florida. On March 26, the president was briefed on the progress of the war and spoke to hundreds of uniformed military personnel. He defended U.S. military strategy, saying, "The path we are taking is not easy and it may be long." Later that night, he met with British Prime Minister Tony Blair at Camp David.

people running around hyperventilating that things aren't going well. We've got a good plan and it's working very, very well."

Meanwhile, in Iraq, nature intervened once again. The sandstorms ended, the sky cleared, and coalition forces were on the move again. This altered the facts on the ground, even as the debate on the airwaves raged on.

Below: An unidentified Iraqi casualty in the bombed-out morgue of a military hospital in Nasiriyah. *Right:* The RFA *Sir Galahad* arrives in Umm Qasr to deliver the first shipment of humanitarian aid.

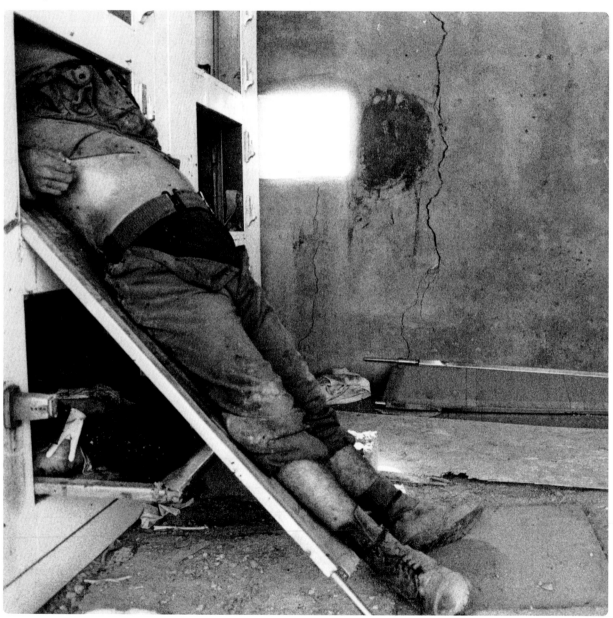

88

HUMANITARIAN AID

GUNS AND BUTTER. *Clockwise from top left:* 82nd Airborne Division paratroopers open boxes of humanitarian rations in Samawah. A child sitting on his father's shoulders fights for food in the southern town of Safwan. A British soldier aboard the *Sir Galahad* after the ship docked on March 28 with food, medicine, and water. A Kuwait Red Crescent delivery is mobbed in southern Iraq. ▨

CHAPTER 6

ROLLING THUNDER

The weather and the pause had unanticipated effects. They allowed the 1st Marine Division to catch up to the leading edge of the northward push. Chip Reid was with the Marines as they headed through central Iraq to the Tigris River and eventually the eastern assault on Baghdad. As they moved, they fought.

"It's when we hit central Iraq that everything changed," Reid recalls. North of Diwaniyah, an ambush led to seven hours of constant fighting. It was "by far the most vicious and difficult and dangerous battle" encountered by the Marines with whom Reid was embedded.

Left: Iraq's network of modern roads made it easier for convoys to move quickly over long distances. *Below:* 1st Marine Division troops at the entry to Kut, south of Baghdad.

93

Even as the sandstorms abated in central Iraq, British forces and Marines around Basra remained stalled. There were reports of a popular uprising and an increasingly critical humanitarian situation.

It was hardly the Marines' first ambush, but earlier, farther south in the Rumaylah oil fields, it had been easier. The Marines were struck then by how poorly trained the Iraqi soldiers actually were. Reid remembers, "They would just kind of wave their guns all over the place. The Marines would take one shot and take out a guy who had been firing his gun wildly for the last few minutes. The guys on the other side couldn't shoot straight. I think that's why the casualty count was pretty low considering the number of times we got ambushed."

For the troops on the ground, the attacks in the south had been "little pinpricks," and they pressed on. Farther north near Diwaniyah, Chip Reid's Marines faced a drastically different enemy. "They didn't surrender, they didn't run, and they could shoot. It was a real war at this point. It wasn't just rolling over them like a steamroller." The reason for the difference became clear once the Marines prevailed.

"Most of the enemy had been dressed in black jumpsuits and were not Iraqi," Reid discovered. "They had passports from Syria, Sudan, Yemen, Jordan, Egypt. Clearly, this was an entirely different element."

In another ambush a bit farther north, Captain Brad Loudon of the 101st Airborne saw exactly what he was facing and realized how brutally the U.S. soldiers would have to respond to enemy forces determined to fight to the death. "These are desperate people doing desperate things in order to survive, and they're throwing everything they've got at us. Soldiers had to do the unimaginable, the unthinkable."

To the west, the 101st Airborne was also getting ambushed as it sought to surround and defeat Ba'ath Party militia, Fedayeen, and security force holdouts near the Shi'ite holy city of Najaf. Like the troops he was with, Dana Lewis had to dive for cover.

"They're sniping," Lewis reported. "They fire and then move to another window or another rooftop. We're lying in ditches trying to find where the fire is coming from. You really don't know where to hide because the bullets echo all over."

Many of the Fedayeen irregulars dressed in civilian clothes, making it difficult to distinguish enemy from noncombatant. The dilemma became clear in Najaf. Lewis recalls a man in civilian dress running

The 101st Airborne Division moved north on March 27 to relieve the 3rd ID at Najaf, positioning itself to the north and south of the city, and eventually taking on the mission of defeating Fedayeen fighters in Karbala as well. Here the division sets up near Kifl and Karbala to root out Iraqi irregulars.

Previous page: Euphrates River crossings at Hindiyah and Musayyib and the Tigris River crossings at Numaniyah remained defended by Republican Guardsmen and were the greatest potential danger zones for moving U.S. heavy equipment. *Above:* In order to clear a path to the Euphrates River bridges, 3rd ID soldiers, here with the 1st Battalion, 30th Infantry, had to search house to house along military routes near Najaf. *Right and far right:* Tens of thousands of Iraqi soldiers shed their uniforms, and Fedayeen militia and other Iraqi regime fighters intentionally blended in with the civilian population, making the job of identifying friendly Iraqi civilians much more difficult for coalition soldiers.

2ND ARMORED CAVALRY REGIMENT DEPARTS FORT POLK, LA.   MARCH 30   GEN. FRANKS DENIES THAT GROUN

out into the open and signaling that there was something wrong with
the ground on which the Marines were walking.

Lewis described the scene as it was happening. "Right now, we've
been told we are walking in the middle of a minefield. Tanks have
already come through here. We're keeping our steps in their tracks,
not moving to either side."

Lewis later recalled that at the time, a U.S. officer had said he
doubted that there was a minefield and suggested that the Iraqi man
was just trying to protect his vegetable field. Ten minutes after he
made the comment, a Humvee drove across the field, hit a mine, and
exploded. Somehow, the two soldiers in the vehicle were unhurt, and
Dana Lewis drew his own conclusion: "The land mines and the man's
friendly warning, two very different examples of the welcome that
may be awaiting U.S. forces farther up the road."

ID MAKES FIRST MAJOR MOVE NORTH IN FIVE DAYS | 101ST AND 82ND AIRBORNE FIGHT TO SECURE NAJAF A

Najaf provided another sort of welcome. At a checkpoint north of town, a suicide bomber posing as a taxi driver killed four soldiers of the 3rd Infantry Division's 1st Brigade.

Iraqi Vice President Taha Yassin Ramadan announced that the tactic would become "routine military policy." Producer Paul Nassar, traveling with the 3rd ID, recalled that from then on the interaction between U.S. soldiers and Iraqi civilians became "much more rigid, much more formal." Nassar had his own reaction. He realized, "Every time Iraqi citizens approached, I had a question in my mind about whether they were going to blow themselves up or not, which is a horrible way to think."

The troops had the same question, of course. Predictably, there were consequences. Troops from the 3rd Infantry Division killed seven civilians, including women and children, who were in a car approaching a checkpoint near Najaf. Central Command later stated that the vehicle had kept moving toward the soldiers "even after warning shots were fired." In another chaotic incident involving the 1st Marine Division, two Iraqi girls were fatally shot. Chip Reid interviewed some of the Marines who fired.

Reid: "What happened that night?"

Marine: "It was a sandstorm day. You couldn't see but thirty meters in front of you. We had seen flashlights in the distance, and

FRONT LINES

On a large scale, only the weather held back the coalition juggernaut. But for each individual soldier on the front lines, the task remained dangerous. *Previous page, top:* A soldier from the 16th Air Assault Brigade outside Basra. *Previous page, bottom:* Members of 3rd Battalion, 5th Marines regiment guard POWs near Nasiriyah. *Left:* Soon after the war began, U.S. military planners shifted the equipment of the 4th ID through the Suez Canal to the Persian Gulf. Turkey had denied permission for the division to cross its soil into northern Iraq. On April 1, division equipment began to arrive in Kuwait ports, meeting up with soldiers flying in from Fort Hood, Texas.

101

Army Green Berets with the 10th Special Forces Group. The Fort Carson, Colorado–based soldiers are high-altitude and mountain specialists.

we were informed that there was enemy out in front of us. When we just fired upon them, we heard . . . children crying."

Another soldier in the group told Reid that a fellow Marine "saw these two guys holding these girls, and as soon as they heard that first shot, they threw the girls in front and ran."

Reid: "So there's no doubt in your mind that they were using these little girls as human shields?"

Marine: "As human shields."

Marine: "It's a psychological war game. The tactics they use, like leaving the little girls' bodies there for us to see in the morning, that was just there to haunt us forever. We're always going to remember that for the rest of our lives."

Trying to come to grips with what happened, one of the Marines said, "It's either them taking our lives or we take their lives." This statement illustrated the type of training and instructions that he and all other troops had received. Just before the war, Major General James N. Mattis, the commander of the 1st Marine Division, had sent a message to all hands:

> "Chemical attack, treachery, and use of the innocent as human shields can be expected, as can other unethical tactics. Take it all in stride. Be the hunter, not the hunted; never allow your unit to be caught with its guard down. Use good judgement and act in best interests of our Nation."

There was a lot to take in stride. NBC cameraman Sebastian Rich had spent many years covering wars and wondered why he thrived in combat. "It sounds incredibly sad, but I don't know how to do anything else," he said. "I mean, I can't fix a car, I don't know how to mend a washing machine, but for some reason, I know how to function in nasty places." Now, in Iraq, Rich spent time with several American snipers and was struck by how matter-of-fact they were when they discussed shooting Iraqi troops. Rich later ran into one of the snipers. "He was in a feeding line handing out food to refugees," Rich remembers, "and he said to me, '[expletive], Sebastian, I don't know where my head is going. I may have killed this woman's husband last night, and now I'm giving her food.'"

Dana Lewis spoke to some soldiers of the 101st Airborne after one especially tough battle. "To one soldier, it was combat fought and won, a victory. Another soldier would shake his head and say, 'I'll never get this out of my head. I've trained to fight tanks in a European war. I didn't train to shoot pickup trucks and soldiers running at me with AK-47s.'"

March 2003

1st Marine Division (REIN)

Commanding General's Message to All Hands

For decades, Saddam Hussein has tortured, imprisoned, raped and murdered the Iraqi people; invaded neighboring countries without provocation; and threatened the world with weapons of mass destruction. The time has come to end his reign of terror. On your young shoulders rest the hopes of mankind.

When I give you the word, together we will cross the Line of Departure, close with those forces that choose to fight, and destroy them. Our fight is not with the Iraqi people, nor is it with members of the Iraqi army who choose to surrender. While we will move swiftly and aggressively against those who resist, we will treat all others with decency, demonstrating chivalry and soldierly compassion for people who have endured a lifetime under Saddam's oppression.

Chemical attack, treachery, and use of the innocent as human shields can be expected, as can other unethical tactics. Take it all in stride. Be the hunter, not the hunted: never allow your unit to be caught with its guard down. Use good judgement and act in best interests of our Nation.

You are part of the world's most feared and trusted force. Engage your brain before you engage your weapon. Share your courage with each other as we enter the uncertain terrain north of the Line of Departure. Keep faith in your comrades on your left and right and Marine Air overhead. Fight with a happy heart and strong spirit.

For the mission's sake, our country's sake, and the sake of the men who carried the Division's colors in past battles-*who fought for life and never lost their nerve*-carry out your mission and *keep your honor clean*. Demonstrate to the world there is "No Better Friend, No Worse Enemy" than a U.S. Marine.

J.N. Mattis
Major General, U.S. Marines
Commanding

Major General James N. Mattis's exhortations to his 1st Marine Division troops at the opening of Operation Iraqi Freedom: "For the mission's sake, our country's sake, and the sake of the men who carried the Division's colors in past battles . . . carry out your mission and keep your honor clean."

Outside Diwaniyah, on March 29, Lieutenant Colonel Carl Mundy, commanding officer of 3rd Battalion, 5th Marines, conducts a battlefield memorial service for Major Kevin Nave and Navy Corpsman Michael Johnson. A pair of M-16 rifles affixed with bayonets and topped with the helmets of the deceased stand in front of the makeshift altar. NBC producer John Zito and cameraman Joe Klimovitz record the ceremony for later air.

There were other factors that led to confusion, mistakes, and accidents. One of them was darkness. Of course, night-vision goggles and other sophisticated equipment gave the coalition an enormous advantage on the battlefield.

However, there were circumstances when that advantage did not apply. For example, troops slept where they stopped, and sometimes there was not enough time for each soldier to dig a foxhole for protection. Using any sort of light was forbidden for security reasons, so it was easy to miss someone asleep on the sand. Marine Major Kevin Nave of the 3/5 was Chip Reid's "go-to guy on any question we had." Nave had longed to be a Marine since he was a kid and wanted to join up right after high school. His parents convinced him to go to college and he did, graduating from the University of Michigan. Then he joined the Marines.

Reid recalls that one day, Major Nave had helped him through the red tape involved in reporting casualties. "Twenty-four hours later," Reid said, "I was using that guidance to report his death. He was run over by an earthmover on one of those nights when it was so dark you couldn't see your hand in front of your face. Even with the night-vision goggles, they didn't see him there." Producer John Zito said, "There was the sense that it shouldn't have happened, although accidents in the battlefield are as much a risk as enemy fire, as much a challenge as engaging the enemy."

Chip Reid noted, "At the memorial service, we were told that when somebody dies on the battlefield, there isn't time to mourn, that you wait until you get back. You just kind of tuck it into a corner of your brain or your soul, and you just leave it there until the end of the war."

Reid did just that, and he addressed Nave's death after the war, privately, instead of during the war, publicly. He reported Nave's death on NBC soon after it happened, but chose to omit the details of how it occurred. When he and producer John Zito got back home weeks later, they visited Nave's family in Michigan. It was then that the family learned all the details of what happened on a very dark night in the Iraqi desert.

IRAQI FAMILIES

A NATION IN NEED. Almost thirteen years of sanctions and more than twenty years of Saddam Hussein's wars took their greatest toll on Iraqi civilians, particularly Iraqi children, who make up 44 percent of the population. Before sanctions, public hospitals in Iraq were free and even 80 percent of rural residents received medical care. Over 90 percent of Iraqis had access to safe water and modern sanitation. The universal education system, which had once been the pride of the Ba'ath Party, lay in shambles after sanctions were implemented. ▨

CHAPTER 7

FIREPOWER

Although there was no way to know it at the time, the war was about half over. As March turned to April, what had been accomplished? What had not? What was there left to do?

On April 2, General Richard Myers, chairman of the Joint Chiefs of Staff, said that 45 percent of Iraq was no longer under Baghdad's control. In the south, British forces were finally making headway in Basra, Iraq's second largest city, where trapped Iraqi officials and irregular forces had been putting up stiff resistance since the start of hostilities.

Bill Neely of ITN, NBC's British partner during the war, reported that Royal Marines used night-vision equipment and superior firepower

Left: Kuwaiti firefighters attempt to extinguish a well fire in the Rumaylah oil fields west of Basra on March 27. *Below:* Air Force A-10 Thunderbolt IIs began operating out of Tallil Air Base in southern Iraq at the end of March, giving them more time over the battlefield.

The Shi'ite mosque and shrine in Najaf. The Ali Mosque holds the tomb of Imam Ali ibn Abu Talib, the Prophet Muhammad's cousin and son-in-law, who is the most beloved saint of Shi'ites.

to push forward toward the city. "They code-named this Operation James, after James Bond, but there was nothing make-believe about it. By dawn, the back of the Iraqi resistance had been broken, but there was no break in the firing."

In central Iraq, the 101st Airborne had reached Najaf, and it came under fire from Iraqi forces taking cover in a holy Shi'ite site, the Ali Mosque. There were strict instructions for coalition troops not to fire on the mosque. Even so, it was a sensitive incident in a sensitive place. Soon after, Najaf citizens almost rioted when they suspected that U.S. troops were heading toward the mosque. A commander instructed the soldiers to kneel and point their weapons at the ground as a signal that no shooting was planned. The troops then withdrew from the area, and the tense moment passed.

Northwest of Baghdad, Special Operations Forces seized the Hadithah dam on the Euphrates River, eliminating coalition concerns that the Iraqis would blow up the dam and flood the Baghdad area.

For days, there was intense fighting between U.S. Army forces and Iraqi defenders. After winning the battle, U.S. troops discovered there were no explosives attached to the dam.

In the north, Iraqi forces continued to retreat while a Special Operations unit called "Task Force Viking" secured the refinery and oil field around Kirkuk. Oil had been discovered there in 1927, and it was the site of the first oil wells ever drilled in the Middle East. Today, there are 337 wells with a capacity to pump 720,000 barrels a day. Coalition forces had feared sabotage and took preventive steps before Task Force Viking even got there; the CIA secretly paid Iraqi guards to protect the refinery. The Kirkuk oil field remained largely undamaged.

All of this happened on the ground, and much of it was visible to cameras and reporters. With one key exception, the war from the air was a different story.

Special Operations troops of JSOTF-N head for the Kirkuk oil fields in northern Iraq.

BAGHDAD BOMBED

Firing cruise missiles and dropping laser- and satellite-guided bombs, the coalition attacked dozens of regime leadership, military, communications, and air defense–related targets in urban Baghdad. Though targets were spread out from Saddam International Airport in the west to the far reaches of eastern Baghdad, the greatest concentration was in the exclusive government sector located in the "elbow" of the Tigris River, an area appropriated for palaces, ministries, and VIP housing, as well as for the offices and barracks of the regime security apparatus.

Azimiyah Palace •

Ministry or

State

Ministr

Special Sec

Mahmoon Comm. Facility •

Mansour

Intelligence Service HQ •

Salam Palace •

Sijood Pa

VIP Hous

Unidentified VIP houses along a man-made peninsula on the Tigris River just south of the Sijood Palace. This satellite photo taken April 1 shows a huge crater where one home used to be near the river and an apparent hole in the ground where an underground bunker may have been hit.

Saddam City

Rusafa

Old City

Fedayeen HQ
•

TV •
tion•
   • Rasheed Street Comm. Facility
zation •   • Presidential Secretariat
inisters •
         Palestine
          Hotel

         • Revolutionary Command Council

lican Palace•
a'ath Party HQ   Regime
                     Sector

Saddam Family   Tigris River
  Residence   • Doura Farms
     •

Above left: The Rasheed Street communications center burns after a B-2 stealth bomber placed a 4,700-pound "bunker buster" inside the building in order to contain external fragments and avoid collateral damage in congested old Baghdad. *Above right:* Uday Hussein's office and the headquarters of the Fedayeen and other volunteer militia in flames. *Far left:* The Council of Ministers, gutted after bombing starting on March 20. In the foreground, the bombed building with the blue dome is the Revolutionary Command Council, Iraq's ruling body. *Below right:* Saddam Hussein's Republican Palace, the traditional palace used mostly for presidential offices and ceremonial meetings.

The Gulf War Air Power Survey called the Mahmoon international telephone exchange ("Al Karkh") at the gates of an upper-middle-class neighborhood in western Baghdad "one of the most important telecommunications facilities in Iraq." The facility was rebuilt after it was bombed in Operation Desert Storm with a new 125-meter-tall "Saddam Tower" with revolving restaurant. The telecommunications center was meticulously attacked to avoid toppling the restaurant tower and damaging nearby civilian homes. *Above:* The Mahmoon facility in 1991 after the Gulf War. *Below:* Defense Department prestrike reconnaissance image. *Bottom:* Poststrike image showing tower still standing. *Right and opposite:* After bombing in 2003.

Baghdad, of course, was one place that could be seen not only by journalists but also by roof-mounted cameras around the city. Offices, palaces, and homes belonging to Saddam Hussein, his family, and the Iraqi inner circle were priority targets. Cameras mounted on the roof of the Palestine Hotel and the Ministry of Information could see the explosions, but the effects of the strikes were anyone's guess. NBC News president Neal Shapiro remembers thinking that one of those cameras might get a stunning shot of a missile headed directly

toward it. "Of course it would be the last image that camera ever transmitted," Shapiro joked.

On March 27 in New York, NBC received the first-ever same-day wartime satellite photographs, material that was available to everyone willing to pay. However, as producer Bob Windrem and NBC military analyst Bill Arkin pored over the huge digital file, they were able to develop information that was not for sale. They could match the buildings, bridges, and other facilities in the photos to installations they had already identified in earlier photos. Therefore, they could determine what, precisely, had been attacked. Windrem realized that "in a subtle way, it changed war coverage" for good. Such material would help journalists deal with military and intelligence officials who always held the advantage of controlling classified information. Within an hour, NBC News was reporting what Arkin and Windrem had identified.

SPECIAL SECURITY OFFICES, BAGHDAD
POST STRIKE

Right: Headquarters of the Special Security Organization in downtown Baghdad, adjacent to the high-rise Planning Ministry. *Below:* A VIP compound on the Tigris River north of Baghdad. Prestrike, the main building and guard quarters are clearly seen. Poststrike, they are obliterated.

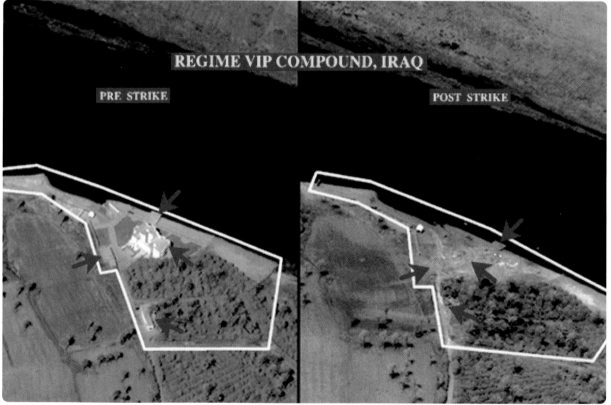

REGIME VIP COMPOUND, IRAQ

PRE STRIKE

POST STRIKE

A Navy F-14A Tomcat is loaded with ordnance during flight operations aboard the USS *Kitty Hawk* in the Persian Gulf on March 30.

The destruction at a Special Security Organization facility was obvious, but most buildings, even those that had been seen burning out of control, showed little apparent damage in the photographs taken from space. The images were deceiving; "bunker-buster" weapons had penetrated the roofs of buildings and exploded inside, leaving few external signs of destruction.

Communications intercepts suggested that the regime was unraveling and increasingly isolated from its military forces.

Vice President Taha Yassin Ramadan, Deputy Prime Minister Tariq Aziz, and the ever-present Information Minister Mohammed al-Sahaf went on TV to reassure Iraqi citizens.

Defense Minister Sultan Hashem Ahmed held a news conference to rally Baghdad's residents. "We will not be surprised if the enemy surrounds Baghdad in five or ten days, but he will have to take the city," he said. "Baghdad cannot be taken as long as the citizens in it are still alive."

Above: Air Force maintenance technicians from Beale Air Force Base in California prepare a U-2 "Dragon Lady" for a high-altitude reconnaissance mission. *Right:* Last-minute preflight checks are performed on an RQ-1 Predator unmanned aerial vehicle. Eighty coalition surveillance aircraft, including fifteen U-2s and nine Predators, took 42,000 images and 3,200 hours of video, placing Iraq under the most intense intelligence microscope ever assembled.

Halfway through the war, coalition aircraft had delivered almost ten thousand strikes. More than two-thirds of those targets were nowhere near television cameras. On March 30, for example, there were more than five hundred strikes on three Republican Guard divisions—the Medina, the Baghdad, and the Hammurabi—deployed south of Baghdad.

Using a high-tech system called "synthetic aperture radar," surveillance planes called JSTARS got a crystal clear picture of the battlefield even through sandstorms. Satellites, high-flying U-2 spy

EUPHRATES RIVER AT MUSAYYIB, 30 MILES FROM DOWNTOWN BAGHDAD | 3RD ID FORCES BEGIN ASSAULT

Aviation ordnance crews move a Joint Stand-Off Weapon (AGM-154) onto the flight deck of the USS *Kitty Hawk*. The version of JSOW used in Iraq delivers 145 cluster bomblets to a range of up to twenty-five miles away. The use of cluster bombs in Iraq was controversial because of the propensity for volatile unexploded bomblets to cause civilian injuries and deaths even after a conflict is over.

planes, tactical reconnaissance planes, and unmanned drones pinpointed each Iraqi tank, missile battery, and troop position.

Air Force, Navy, Marine Corps, and Royal Air Force bombers and pilots received the targeting data and unleashed deadly accurate strikes.

Ironically, bad weather probably helped this effort. As Pentagon correspondent Jim Miklaszewski pointed out, "Radio intercepts showed that Iraqis thought the sandstorms that halted ground troops would also provide protective cover from the air." They were wrong. According to Miklaszewski, U.S. air commanders could not believe what happened next.

"The Iraqis were actually trying to reinforce the Medina division," explained one official. "Troops from other Republican Guard divisions were sent south. Once on the road, they became even easier targets. We couldn't believe it. It was a slaughter."

By the end of March, intelligence analysts concluded that the Medina division was only 20 percent combat effective, with no

On March 26, the worst single reported instance of civilian deaths in Baghdad occurred in the Sha'ab neighborhood. Some fourteen civilians were killed and thirty injured on a shopping street, according to Iraqi officials. U.S. military sources suggested that an Iraqi missile may have gone astray and caused the damage. Later, Marine Captain Ryan "Irish" deMik and his comrades found an example of an Iraqi surface-to-air missile that evidently fell back to earth and hit a building near Baghdad.

chance for reinforcement. U.S. military officials estimated that in the Medina division strikes alone, thousands of Iraqi troops were killed.

Another incident, in which initial reports said that fourteen Iraqis were killed, attracted much more attention. The dead, along with dozens of injured, were civilians. The incident constituted the worst reported instance of civilian casualties in the war. It happened in Baghdad, where cameras were near, on a shopping street in the northern neighborhood of Sha'ab. Iraqi officials and Baghdad residents blamed it on an American missile strike. U.S. officials said they did not know what happened and raised the possibility that the cause could have been an Iraqi surface-to-air missile gone astray. The question still has not been resolved.

More than bombs were raining down on the Iraqis. A classified flight mission called "Commando Solo" broadcast a mix of anti-Saddam messages and popular music. Correspondent Kelly O'Donnell got aboard. "A dark and noisy radio and TV station in the sky, the plane carries eleven antennas that simultaneously transmit

Below: NBC correspondent Kelly O'Donnell on board the "Commando Solo" broadcast plane, circling over Iraq. *Bottom:* Aviation ordnance crews prepare GBU-12 five-hundred-pound laser-guided bombs aboard the aircraft carrier USS *Theodore Roosevelt* on March 27.

123

Right: A Marine Corps F/A-18C Hornet taxis during a sandstorm at Jaber Air Base in Kuwait on March 26. Air operations continued during the storm, focusing a majority of the bombing on the Republican Guard divisions south of Baghdad. *Bottom:* Crew chiefs with the 392nd Air Expeditionary Wing conduct pre-flight checks on an A-10, affectionately known as the "Warthog." Two hundred and fifty F/A-18s and sixty Warthogs flew during Operation Iraqi Freedom.

different radio and TV channels during secret routes across Iraq, easily tuned in on the ground."

Millions of propaganda leaflets dropped by U.S. aircraft supplemented the Commando Solo broadcasts and other clandestine radio signals.

Iraqi propaganda efforts were much more low-tech, but they succeeded in preserving the mystery of Saddam Hussein's health and whereabouts. Saddam appeared on TV several times, and each occasion prompted another round of questions. NBC's Andrea Mitchell tracked the "Where is Saddam?" story:

March 22: "The question—where is Saddam Hussein? Why isn't he emerging to prove his regime is intact?"

March 24: "U.S. officials tell NBC News that voice-print technology confirms the man on today's videotape was Saddam Hussein. Although the tape is edited, Saddam refers to fighting in Basra."

April 4: "Intelligence officials say it appears to be Saddam Hussein, defiant even as coalition forces encircle Baghdad. Looking more like a politician at a campaign stop than a besieged dictator. If it is Saddam, it would be his first public appearance in years."

In interviews and appearances on TV, other Iraqi officials maintained an air of normalcy and optimism. Iraqi Foreign Minister Naji Sabri told the BBC, "The president is well; the leadership are well and functioning normally." At another point, Sabri said that only surrender would save U.S. and British troops from a "holocaust."

And Information Minister al-Sahaf told Iraqis to strike back— hard. "Hit them. Fight them. They are cursed. They are evil. We will be victorious and they will be defeated. Fight them everywhere. Don't give them a chance to breathe until they withdraw and retreat."

By this time back in the States, late-night comedians were using al-Sahaf's statements in their stand-up routines, referring to him as "Baghdad Bob" and "Comical Ali." It did not appear that coalition forces were taking him very seriously, either.

Iraqi television aired images of Saddam Hussein on April 4 showing the Iraqi president walking on a Baghdad street with a small entourage, presumably in or near the Mansour neighborhood west of his palace enclave.

BAGHDAD DESTROYED

ON TARGET. By the end of Operation Iraqi Freedom, coalition forces had dropped 19,948 guided and 9,251 unguided weapons, about the same percentage of smart weapons employed in Afghanistan and twice that of the 1999 Yugoslav War. In Operation Desert Storm in 1991, the coalition dropped 225,000 weapons, some 8 percent of which were precision guided. ▨

CHAPTER 8

CLOSE QUARTERS

As the war developed, so did the relationships between embedded journalists and the soldiers they were covering. The military had set the tone much earlier; coverage was to be uncensored and unimpeded, whatever the story. As stated in *Ground Rules for Media*, "These ground rules recognize the right of the media to cover military operations and are in no way intended to prevent release of derogatory, embarrassing, negative, or uncomplimentary information."

Left: 3rd ID soldiers at the front in southern Iraq.
Below: NBC cameraman Craig White and engineer Robert Lapp with Lieutenant Colonel Stephen Twitty, commander, 3rd Battalion, 15th Infantry.

PHIL ALONGI

Executive Director, Specials Planning

"When I first heard about the embed proposal, I was skeptical. After seeing it in action from 5 A.M. to 11 P.M., day in and day out, I became a believer. In my view, what really made it a success was the resourcefulness of the NBC News men and women assigned to these positions. I knew that when presented with a difficult situation, they would make it work for all parties involved. I was privileged to work with such a brave group of people for those very long hours."

Above: NBC Cameraman Joe Klimovitz, *foreground,* with the 3rd Battalion, 5th Marines, as they move into Ash Shumali south of Baghdad. *Right:* Press passes of, *clockwise,* Craig White, Kerry Sanders, Dana Lewis, Robert Grant, Chip Reid, Tom Aspell.

The military had good reason to favor embedding. NBC's Pentagon producer Tammy Kupperman pointed out that in Afghanistan, the military had been stung time and again by charges of civilian casualties and raids gone bad. "The Pentagon," she added, "was keenly aware of these constant claims, some of which were true and others false. Internally, some officers made the case that the best defense in most situations would be to have independent journalists there at the raids to observe and report what they saw."

Pentagon correspondent Jim Miklaszewski also felt that embedding was not motivated by the desire to do the press a favor. "The Pentagon decision to embed reporters was not made in the name of First Amendment freedoms or a strong desire to provide news organizations and the American public with a front-row seat to the war. It was made primarily because Pentagon officials saw this as the best way to combat possible psychological warfare and propaganda by the Saddam Hussein regime."

"For me, the most enduring image of this war was the face of U.S. Army Specialist Shoshana Johnson in her first hours as a prisoner of war. Was it fear I saw reflected in her eyes? Confusion? Who was behind the camera pressing her for answers? What was she seeing that we couldn't? And if her family was watching this videotape, what must they be thinking? All of those questions raced through my mind as the tape played out. This was the war—brought home—suddenly, startlingly, in the face of one American soldier.

"That same night, I interviewed Johnson's parents in their living room in El Paso, Texas. What came through to me as I spoke with them was not fear, but personal strength, faith in the Almighty, and an unshakeable belief that their daughter would come home safely. As time passed, there was little to encourage them. But the Johnsons' faith was well placed. Three weeks later, I was back in El Paso interviewing them again, this time on the happiest of occasions. Shana and her comrades had been rescued. Soon, they'd be home.

"They say all politics is local. You can look at war that way, too. No matter how large the conflict, no matter how many thousands of soldiers are involved, war's impact is best measured in the lives of a community, a family, a mother, and a father."

Predictably, there were mutual suspicions at the beginning of the war. Dana Lewis recalls asking a lieutenant colonel how he had felt when he learned that an NBC News team was coming along. The officer said he had turned to his colonel and remarked, "Well, why don't we just invite the Iraqi enemy into our planning tent as well?"

The journalists had qualms, too. Thirty-two-year-old producer John Zito had covered the war in Afghanistan, the Israeli-Palestinian conflict, and stories in Iran, Syria, Lebanon, and Jordan before arriving in Iraq. He remembers his concerns about embedding with the troops, that the journalists should not become one of "them." Reporters had to constantly remind themselves that they were just there to observe and document. "Observing and reporting objectively—this was journalism's mission," said Zito.

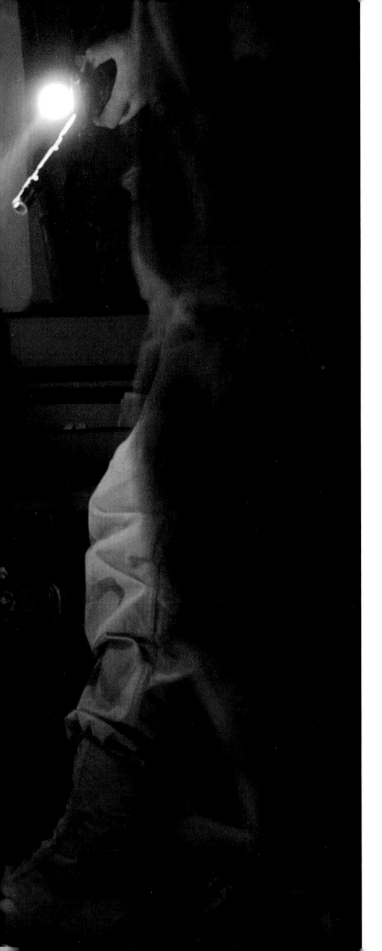

Mail from home is still instant therapy for the troops. The bounty of books, baby wipes, photos, snacks, foot powder, lip balm, cigarettes, and audiotapes often arrived weeks late and battered from the arduous trip.

LESTER HOLT

Anchor and Correspondent

"Although I knew that our correspondents were providing an accurate, unflinching account of the action, I was keenly aware that their view of this war was sharply limited to what was happening around them. I was compelled to remind our viewers that they were essentially seeing the war through a soda straw. I was concerned that the amazing access we experienced through our embedded correspondents was creating unrealistic expectations. No one embedded journalist could provide the big picture of how the war was going—only vivid snapshots. As the war went on, we all began to better understand their role, which was to give us the soldier's or Marine's perspective and to personalize something as impersonal as war.

"As an anchor, my difficult task was to piece together how the battle in Nasiriyah that Kerry Sanders had just described related to the action that Chip Reid or David Bloom were reporting somewhere else and what it all meant for the question, 'How is the war going?' "

But being together with the troops under difficult and dangerous conditions changed the psychological equation, and Zito knew it. "The bond got stronger the more time you spent with them going through more horrid experiences. It was a real challenge editorially because at the beginning of every report, you had to constantly separate the words 'I' and 'we.' So whatever the military's intentions were in sending us out there, it was probably the smartest thing they could have done, because naturally you grow more sensitive to the subjects if you're depending on them."

As the journalists warmed to the soldiers, the soldiers warmed to the journalists. Cameraman Craig White observed, "At first, the military was very skeptical of us, but that dissipated quickly. I think that soldiers saw journalists as having somewhat the same gene pool. We had a mission that was very similar to theirs. They were going to fight a war. We were going to cover a war. Those goals are not necessarily mutually exclusive."

Correspondent Dana Lewis got what he called "incredible access" to the workings of the 101st Airborne, including top-secret briefings in the field. He was part of the first true test of the embed process, an episode involving what the media ground rules called "embarrassing, negative, uncomplimentary information."

"Fragging" or attempted murder of fellow soldiers, is perhaps the most troubling act that any soldier can imagine. In this case, a disgruntled soldier allegedly tossed grenades and fired shots at his superior officers. Two died and fourteen were injured. When the incident occurred near the Kuwait-Iraq border, a CBS camera was closest, and it recorded the capture of the soldier accused of the fragging. The videotape was made available to other news organizations, including NBC, and the question was "Would the military allow the prompt transmission of that tape?" The answer was yes. All the broadcast and cable networks received it promptly and put it on television.

The next day brought a twist to the story. Dana Lewis was denied access to a memorial service for an officer killed in the fragging. When Lewis protested, a colonel told him, "Look, the story is a day old and we have a war to fight. I can't imagine why you're still reporting that." Lewis found the exchange instructive.

"The colonel never tried to stop us from reporting, but the incident demonstrated one way of controlling reports coming from embeds," he said. "The Army won't censor our material, but it can and will control what we get access to. We rely on their transportation and their goodwill to get us where we want to go, and sometimes they are not interested in providing access to what we think is news."

CHRIS MATTHEWS

Host, *Hardball with Chris Matthews*

"The reports coming from the embedded teams during the war were astonishing, giving Americans everywhere a vivid picture of war in the twenty-first century. Our challenge now is to sustain that intensity as we cover what is perhaps a bigger challenge than the war itself: the occupation and the restoration of the Iraqi nation."

Opposite left: NBC military analyst Bill Arkin briefs Tom Brokaw on the war's progress. *Below:* Chip Reid, *right,* talks with Sergeant Major Joe Vines of 3/5 Marines, *left,* and Lieutenant Colonel Carl Mundy, battalion commander, *center.*

The fragging incident came up on NBC's *Meet the Press*, where Tim Russert's guest was Defense Secretary Donald Rumsfeld. "You know, it's interesting," Rumsfeld said. "Here we have permitted press people to be embedded, as they say, with the overwhelming majority of our elements—air, land, and sea. And so what happens is, we see an image like that."

General Tommy Franks, the coalition commander of the war, was less concerned about images shown than information revealed. Jim Miklaszewski observed that two days into the war, Franks was worried that too many details about U.S. troop movements were being reported.

He ordered a news blackout, which came as a surprise to Pentagon officials, especially Torie Clarke, assistant secretary of state for public affairs. As Miklaszewski put it, "The embedding process was her baby." Immediately, Clarke appealed to Defense Secretary Rumsfeld to overrule Franks. The blackout order was rescinded several hours later.

Troops on the ground were also eager for coverage, even of unfortunate incidents. In Nasiriyah, a group of Marines separated from the main unit fired on their fellow soldiers, under a mistaken impression of where enemy forces were located. The friendly fire incident left thirty-one Marines wounded, and Kerry Sanders noted that the troops involved actively encouraged him to report the story.

"They call it 'blue on blue,' and in many ways it's embarrassing to the military," said Sanders. "But the Marines wanted that story told. They were not embarrassed to let a journalist tell the bad and the ugly because their true desire was to make sure it never happened again."

Sanders recalls that some of the Marines took a bit of heat from back home. "They got calls from Camp Lejeune asking why they had let the media go there. The response was, 'Shouldn't your first question be about the thirty-one people who were injured?' It told me a lot right there."

Certainly, there were times when the interests of the military and the media coincided. Sanders was involved in one such incident when wounded Marines on stretchers passed right behind him as he was giving a live report on *Today* from Nasiriyah.

Moments later, Sanders videotaped an interview with Lance Corporal Joshua Menard, who had been wounded in the hand. When Sanders had finished, unaware that cameraman Sebastian Rich was still videotaping, he offered Menard his satellite phone to call home. Sanders reflects, "Giving him the phone, I never thought, 'Okay, I'm a reporter. I don't influence a situation—I stand back.' To me, it was more a matter of one human being to another."

The impact was huge and almost instantaneous. Menard's mother had been watching *Today* when the stretchers passed behind Sanders giving his live report. She thought she saw her son but wasn't certain. Then came the phone call, and the reunion was further dramatized by the fact that Joshua's mother was a nurse. She gave her professional assessment of his wound. And it all played on TV.

TIM RUSSERT

Moderator, *Meet the Press*, and Washington Bureau Chief

"For the media, covering a war is not analogous to reporting on a political campaign or tax-cut debate. At NBC, we spent long hours discussing this challenge. For myself, I concluded that when covering military operations, the media should modulate its tone.

"Indeed, the press and the government will have robust disagreements over what is fair and timely and relevant news coverage, even how to define 'national security.' We should, of course, provide coverage to those who dissent from official government policy. To be able to disagree, even with the president of the United States, is central to who we are as a people and a nation. But we must never report anything that puts our troops at risk, and we must always reject any attempt to suggest a moral equivalency between the United States of America and terrorists. We may be journalists, but we are also American citizens."

WENDY WILKINSON

Deputy Bureau Chief, Washington

"In the end, the embeds worked well because the directives that came from Torie Clarke and her team were further enhanced by the military leadership in the field. Those leaders came to know our embeds as sincere and dedicated men and women determined to tell the story right. The military helped us get where we needed to go and gave us a lot of factual information we needed to flesh out our reports. They gave us part of themselves in every broadcast we did along the way to Baghdad."

ANDREA MITCHELL

Chief Foreign Affairs Correspondent

"Covering wartime intelligence and diplomacy seemed to mirror the challenge of getting the story 'right' that our people in the field were confronting. Our sources were mostly U.S. officials, often unable or unwilling to let me use their names. Even though I constantly tested their information against what foreign diplomats and U.N. officials were telling me, I was always concerned that we were being used. When a CIA analyst tells me Saddam appears injured on a video, is that disinformation to demoralize the Iraqi leadership? I often felt as though I was walking through a hall of mirrors, relying on trusted sources but always worrying that we didn't have enough independent ways to make sure we weren't part of *their* agenda.

"As I watched Kerry, Dana, Chip, David, and my other embedded colleagues, I thought about all the arguments I've participated in about sending broadcasters into conflicts from Grenada to the first Gulf War and Panama. Endless debates over whether television would compromise combat operations were finally resolved. Both sides learned so many lessons about our separate missions. There was a lot of White House choreography in the daily Centcom briefings, but when it came to reports from the field, it seemed as though the media and the military both figured out how to communicate reality without artifice and without putting the troops or their families at greater physical or emotional risk."

Kerry Sanders said later, "So much of what people see on television seems to be created and organized and calculated. This war was not calculated. Whatever happened right in front of you became the story you told. You didn't know what was going to happen. There was no predictability."

It was predictable, however, that there would be wounded soldiers whose battlefield stories the Pentagon wanted reported. By having reporters and cameras in places where they would encounter the wounded, it became a certainty that many of those stories would be told. If it hadn't been Kerry Sanders and Joshua Menard, it would have been another reporter and another wounded soldier. So two agendas were served: Television told the stories it wanted to tell, and the military provided access to the stories it wanted told.

This symbiosis culminated in the most celebrated "human" story of the war: the rescue of Private First Class Jessica Lynch. At half

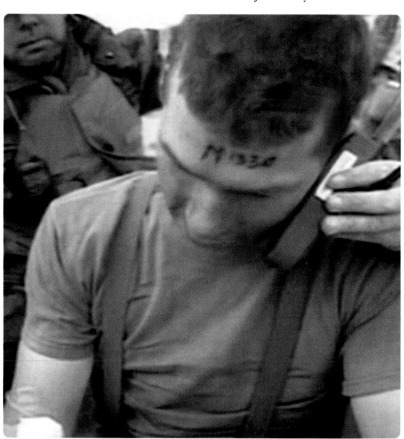

Joshua Menard talks to his mother after she watched him on *Today*.

past midnight on April 2, Special Forces commandos stormed a hospital in Nasiriyah, nine days after Lynch and fourteen other soldiers had disappeared.

Several days before the rescue, Fox Company of the Marine's Task Force Tarawa had raided a different hospital. As the Marines searched the building, they found chemical protection suits, masks, and bloody American uniforms with the flags and name patches torn off. In one room, they found a car battery with electrical wires leading to a bed frame, prompting strong suspicions that torture had been practiced there. But they found no Americans, alive or dead.

For days, the trail stayed cold until an Iraqi civilian, a lawyer named Mohammed Odeh al-Rehaief, reportedly approached the Marines and told them that an American woman was in a hospital on the east bank of the Euphrates River. At the urging of the Marines, he agreed to make several more trips to the hospital, where his wife

MARK EFFRON
Vice President, Live News Programming, MSNBC

"Some of the most vivid and memorable journalism from our embedded reporters showed up on MSNBC in the middle of the night. There were fewer time restrictions and more opportunities for unfettered storytelling, and there were times when I would close my eyes and just listen. It hearkened back to the memorable radio coverage of World War II I had read about. There was an intimacy to their reporting that made you feel you were there with them."

NBC cameraman Joe Klimovitz in Ash Shumali.

139

DAVID VERDI
Executive News Director

"We realized from the very start that the viewers' expectation for coverage was 'live,' but not the old way, with big, bulky satellite uplinks that limited our ability to travel, or even the new way, with grainy, jumpy videophone technology. We needed unique, extremely portable broadcast-quality uplinks that we could move around the theater in real time. Such technology didn't exist. So when the Pentagon floated the embedding idea, the heat was on to create new equipment. It was a thrilling race against the clock, with components rolling off the assembly line to be shipped to Kuwait, Jordan, and Iraq right up to the start of the war. I imagine this is what the military feels when it is desperately trying to deploy a new weapon before battle begins.

"I wasn't sure the Bloommobile would work. There were too many variables, and it was only tested on the streets of Florida where it was built. David's opening shot on *Today* wearing goggles and helmet with his hair blowing in the wind and the desert flowing past behind him took us all—and our competitors—by surprise. It looked like a shot from a movie. It showed, for the first time live and in broadcast quality, what it was like to be riding a military vehicle to battle. We were speechless."

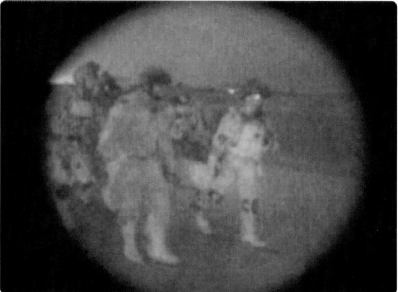

Centcom-supplied images of the nighttime rescue of Private First Class Jessica Lynch, which proved to be one of the most controversial news stories of the war.

was a nurse, and draw diagrams of the building, including the location of the room occupied by the American.

At about the same time, an Iraqi man who spoke English approached Kerry Sanders. "He asked me, 'You journalists?' And I said, 'Yeah.' And he goes, 'You have to know there's an American being held at the hospital; she's being tortured; she needs to be rescued. Make sure the military authorities know this.'"

Sanders never could determine whether this was the same man

who had tipped off U.S. forces, but he relayed the information to the Marines, who said they already knew it. Several nights later, after Special Forces began appearing, Sanders was invited to a meeting in the tactical area.

"They said, 'Kerry, it's going down tonight. Special Forces is going in, and they're going to rescue Jessica Lynch. It's going to happen at 12:30 tonight. Obviously, you can't report anything about this.'"

Sanders asked about the best location for him and cameraman Sebastian Rich. They were guided to a bridge with a clear view of Ba'ath Party headquarters, located near the hospital. An attack on the headquarters would be a diversionary tactic during the rescue mission.

For cameraman Sebastian Rich, it was a new experience. "It was funny, because for the first time ever in my life, I knew exactly where to point the camera before the battle started. I had a staff sergeant with night-vision goggles saying, 'Pan your camera two degrees over there'—and at whatever time it was—'turn your camera on.' And there it was. A battle just erupted in front of the camera."

In television terminology, this is "the wide shot." At about the same time, a Special Forces cameraman entered the hospital with the rescue team. He videotaped the dramatic close-ups that soon became famous and later prompted questions about whether the commando

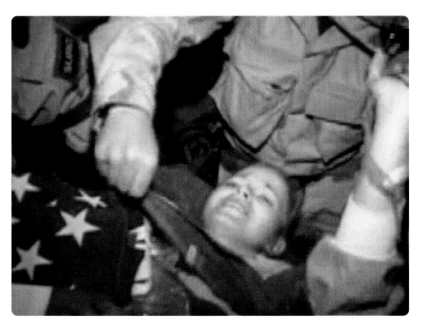

STACY BRADY

Vice President, Network News Field and Satellite Operations

"We started planning for the war in September, making daily calls about people, equipment, and logistics. It was an exhausting process because the 'plan' changed daily. Who's going where, when are they going, who are they going with, do they need night-vision goggles, did they get CBR [chemical, biological, radiological] training, do they have a laptop, and on and on. We had enormous spreadsheets tracking all these details.

"Finally, David Verdi told us to start moving people and equipment into place, and we deployed. Someone from ABC spotted the Bloommobile and thought it was a giant microwave truck. CBS called to try and figure out what technology we were using.

"Then, bam! We were on the air. The pictures were beautiful, the audio crisp, everything was working. I watched David Bloom driving through the desert and thought to myself, 'How cool is that!'

"Already, it seems like a long time ago, but when I see all the sand left in our gear, it's evident how recent it was."

HODA KOTB

Correspondent, *Dateline NBC*

"Embeds were protected by the military, but those of us who went into Baghdad on our own were left to protect ourselves. I went in after the fall of the statue when I imagined things would be calm, but it was more like the Wild West.

"Being an Egyptian-American woman helped me out tremendously. It was handy to know phrases in Arabic that often diffused very tense situations."

TOM TOUCHET

Executive Producer, *Today*

"The war in Iraq was by far the most challenging event *Today* had ever faced, and much of the war news ended up breaking on our watch: the rush through the desert seen through David Bloom's camera, the battle of Nasiriyah, the sandstorms, the statue falling in Baghdad. Seeing the events unfold, reacting to them, and putting them into context often happened while we were live on the air. This meant constant choices and decisions and an enormous responsibility for Katie and Matt and the rest of our *Today* team. There was no precedent to follow."

Above: NBC's adopted "Seven Ton" compliments of 2nd Battalion, 8th Marines.

team had overdramatized the rescue. There were claims that the team had information that enemy troops were no longer present, but those claims were never proved. Sanders thinks that it would not have made a difference.

"Based on what I know as a reporter and what I've observed about the way the military operates, even if they were told that there was no Iraqi military in there, the approach to enter that hospital would not have been any different. That's because the intelligence they gathered was so often wrong."

The issue of inaccurate intelligence had come up before the 507th Maintenance Company got into trouble and before Sanders's Marine unit had even arrived in Nasiriyah. Sanders recalls a young Marine captain expressing surprise that NBC would want to accompany the Marines into the town. "We're not going to see any action," Sanders remembers him saying. "Nasiriyah will be quiet." Later, after all hell broke loose, the same captain told Sanders, "So much for the intel. So much for knowing where any of Saddam's army is."

Central Command released a five-minute edited version of the Special Operations mission to rescue Jessica Lynch. It did not release the unedited footage, despite repeated requests for it.

As for Jessica Lynch, many questions remained unanswered long after she was rescued. There were reports, later discounted, that she sustained bullet and knife wounds when she was first taken. Other reports said she was injured because her Humvee went out of control and collided with another U.S. vehicle. Lynch suffered compression of the spine and multiple fractures of her ribs, a shoulder, an arm, a leg, and a foot. There were reports that she fired her weapon at enemy troops, while a later report said her weapon jammed. Other reports said the accident knocked her unconscious. It remained unclear if she was a prisoner or just a patient in the hospital where she was found. The bodies of eight U.S. soldiers missing since March 23 were also discovered at the hospital. Later that same night, Central Command held a briefing in Qatar. The briefer, Brigadier General Vincent Brooks, used the word "retrieved" to describe the commandos' action when they brought Lynch back into American hands.

On May 8, Lynch's physician, Army Doctor Greg Argyros, appeared on *Today* and said, "She has no memory whatsoever of any of the events from the time her convoy came under attack until she woke up in the Iraqi hospital."

The Jessica Lynch saga was surely the most scrutinized story of the war. While hundreds, perhaps thousands, of embedded reports

LUZ ELENA TORRES

Producer and Photographer, Telemundo Network News

"Although there were countless moments of misery—no decent water, lack of hygienic facilities, hot temperatures, sand everywhere, pesky mosquitoes, lack of sleep, and more—I would not trade this experience for anything. The soldiers I met made up for all the inconveniences, and the best reward was being able to give them time with their families. The videophone was such a hit, letting soldiers send love to their families on camera. We soon realized that there were Hispanics from everywhere. We met Puerto Ricans, Mexicans, Chileans, Argentineans, Colombians, Cubans, Salvadorans, Hondurans, Guatemalans, Ecuadorans, even Costa Ricans. A few had yet to receive their U.S. citizenship."

DANNY NOA

Director, Foreign News

"The embed ordeal was a bumpy ride. The Pentagon would say one thing, the field officers something else. Our folks in Kuwait just put their heads down and busted through, making whatever deals they could. In the end it was the producers, correspondents, and techs in Kuwait who really saved the day. They made sure we got in with the necessary equipment. It was an ordeal all right, but I'm glad we had these guys on our side."

3/5 Marines calling in air, artillery, and mortar support aboard a command vehicle in southern Iraq.

143

DAVID CORVO

Executive Producer, *Dateline NBC*

"As a producer in New York who put the embeds and their material on the air, I was keenly aware that they had a limited field of vision. As they told us over and over, they could only report what they saw and learned firsthand. It was important that the audience know that, so we were very specific in our language when introducing their reports. Nevertheless, they gave millions of viewers an understanding of the soldier's life that was undeniably authentic—and breathtaking."

came and went without much notice, media analysts, journalists, and others followed the Lynch story and dissected the coverage long after the war was over. Several months after the rescue, Sebastian Rich reflected on being an embedded journalist.

"I'm still not convinced about the embed process. I personally would like to be more detached. But having said that, from a cameraman's point of view, my God, what pictures. Take out everything else, but just from a purely professional selfish point of view, fantastic pictures."

Kerry Sanders, however, remains a staunch defender of embedding. "Taken as a whole, I don't understand how anybody would want to criticize us for getting too close. The reason this worked so well was that there was no minder there. There was nobody saying, 'Okay, show them this. We want this image. We want that image.'"

Jim Miklaszewski is also a strong supporter of the embed process. "For me, the embedded reporters were a godsend," he says. "My job was to provide a 'big picture' overview of the day's events on the battlefield. Embedded reporters were my own personal army. Almost every report included a dramatic, first-person account from our correspondents."

The value of those accounts depended on the correspondents separating the "I" from the "we." Producer John Zito observed that it was crucial to maintain some critical distance from the soldiers. Sometimes that was easy. Sometimes it wasn't. It was unpredictable. Just like war.

Opposite left: A helicopter waits to transport a wounded soldier for treatment. *Below:* NBC correspondent Jim Maceda questions a military officer in Baghdad.

145

SOLDIER LIFE

IT TAKES ALL TYPES. *Clockwise from top left:* Coast Guard reservist Taurean Cooper brushes his teeth at the Mina al-Bakr oil terminal. A female soldier searches an Iraqi woman before allowing her to get into an ambulance near Nasiriyah. A Marine sleeps close to his weapon. Navy Ensign Katharine Poole watches for surface contacts on board the guided-missile cruiser USS *Shiloh. Next page, top:* Marine Corporal Gunnar Schmitt found "Willie" in Baghdad. *Right:* Army Specialists George Gillette and Robert Boucher enjoy a swim in an irrigation pond. *Bottom left:* For most soldiers and Marines, the buzz cut was welcome. *Following page:* Specialists Tonya Stevenson and Jenn Dietsch eat breakfast at the Forward Ammo and Refueling Point (FARP) Shell. *Following page, left:* Soldiers used plastic bags to protect their rifles and equipment from blowing sand and dust. *Below left:* Any contraption was welcome for a good night's sleep. *Right:* Foot care is still an essential chore for those in uniform. ▧

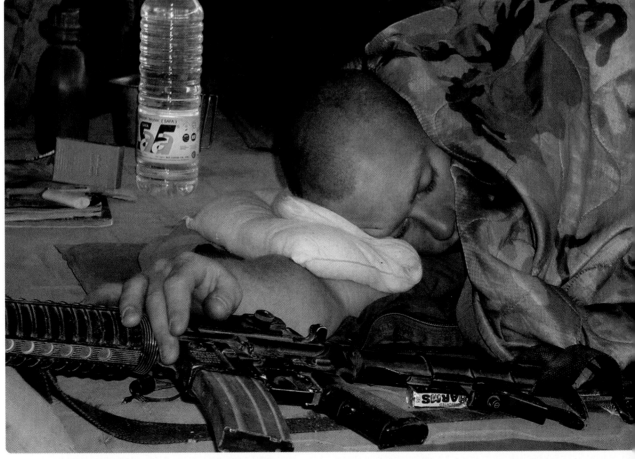

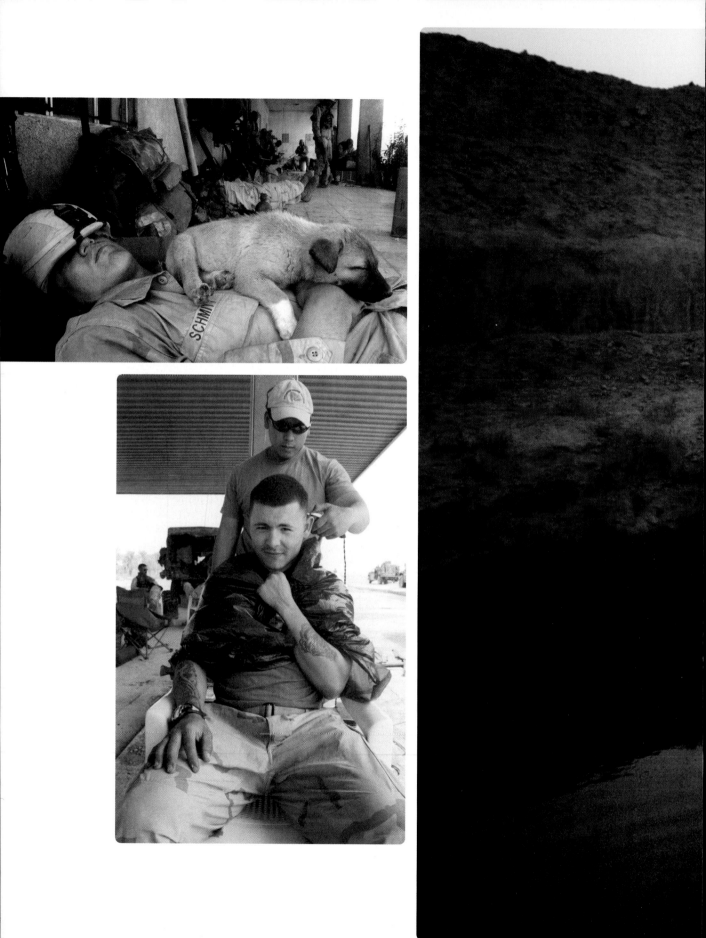

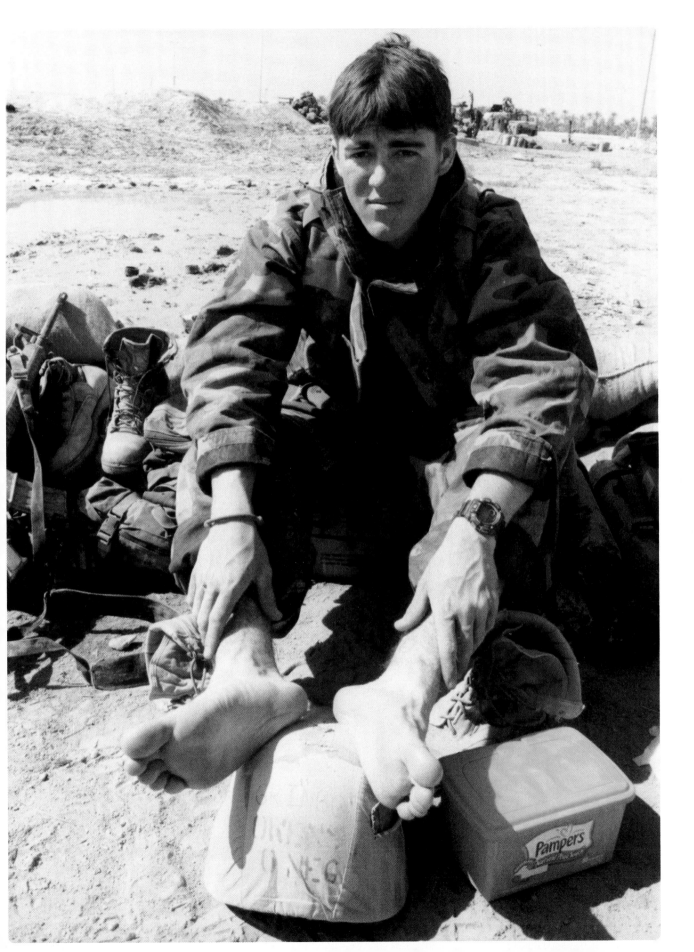

CHAPTER 9

CROSSING THE LINE

An imaginary and imprecise line stretches from just south of Karbala across to Kut, in eastern Iraq. The coalition called it the "red line." It was some fifty miles south of downtown Baghdad, and the feeling among the troops was that if Iraq was going to use chemical or biological weapons at all, it would be when coalition forces crossed that line.

The warning alarms had been going off since the war's beginning, when Iraq fired missiles into Kuwait. One week into the war, NBC analyst David Kay, who had been a United Nations weapons inspector in Iraq during the 1990s, told Tom Brokaw, "What I'm worried about are the increasing signs of chem capability that we're seeing. I think that's what is really fearsome as we move and close in on Baghdad."

All through the northward push toward the city, with each discovery of some huge weapons cache—and there were many such discoveries—

Far left: Colonel Steve Hummer, commander of the 7th Marine Regiment, and Lieutenant Colonel Bryan McCoy, commander of the 3rd Battalion, 4th Marines, pore over maps of Baghdad as they plan the regiment's attack on the capital. *Left:* Combat vehicle nicknames like "Blood Mary" or "Terminator" are common. Commanders are always trying to keep the troops from being too "colorful" in their descriptions.

155

the alarming question was posed anew: Is this where we will find WMD, weapons of mass destruction? Each alarm was false.

Dana Lewis, for example, caught up to the 101st Airborne's strike brigade at a fertilizer plant east of Karbala. Wearing gas masks, the troops uncovered a pit and found twenty-five-gallon and fifty-five-gallon drums, fourteen in all. Lewis reported, "Preliminary tests, which often prove to be false, found a deadly cocktail of possible sarin and tabun nerve agent, as well as a mustard agent known as lewisite."

David Kay suggested caution, saying, "There's reason to be suspicious, but you also want to be very confident before you announce that you've found a smoking gun."

Soldiers with the 3rd ID take cover as they survey Iraqi positions in a village across the Euphrates River on their approach to Baghdad.

156

Saddam's troops. Up until the last few days, Iraqi forces stood guard on the outskirts of Baghdad.

It was not a smoking gun. Well after the preliminary tests, subsequent analysis showed the drums contained only industrial chemicals. Until the final results were known, however, Lewis and his cameraman, Bill Angelucci, were shaken. Lewis said, "We were caught without full chemical gear and not well protected if this was a real danger. I tried to stay upwind. We tried to be careful, but we knew we were taking a risk."

So every precaution was taken as U.S. forces prepared to cross the red line. After Marine forces captured an important Tigris River crossing at Numaniyah, troops with the 3rd Battalion, 7th Marine donned chemical suits as they entered the red zone.

To the west, the Army's V Corps, led by the 3rd Infantry Division, prepared to cross an area called the Karbala gap, between the town of Karbala and Lake Razzazah, on its way toward Saddam International Airport in western Baghdad. The topography forced the troops to travel single-file across raised embankments, a situation that

Republican Guardsmen on the outskirts of Baghdad on April 3. Their heavy equipment, *right,* had been decimated further south; even as Saddam International Airport was falling, soldiers continued to man their positions in Baghdad.

presented great danger. In fact, great danger was the working assumption among all the Army and Marine troops now inside the red zone. They were finally expecting to confront the elite Republican Guard troops about whom they had heard so much. To reach Baghdad, coalition forces would have to fight through Iraq's best equipped and best trained units. Or so they thought.

Above: U.S. Marines found these two missiles near Madbutryah in central Iraq on March 31. Iraq had started destroying longer-range versions of these same Al Samoud missiles before the war after U.N. inspectors concluded that they exceeded the maximum allowable range of 150 kilometers. *Left:* A weapons cache near Karbala. Similar huge stores of military hardware were found throughout the country.

The Pentagon sought to lower expectations. Major General Stanley McChrystal, Joint Staff operations chief, said, "We are planning for a very difficult fight ahead in Baghdad. We are not expecting to drive into the city suddenly and seize it."

But once again, things did not turn out as expected. Although there were some intense firefights, especially involving the 1st Marine Division as it approached the southeastern outskirts of Baghdad, the Iraqi resistance was far weaker than expected. Not enough Iraqi troops and equipment had survived to wage what Saddam, in the Gulf War twelve years earlier, had called the "mother of all battles." The reason was as clear as the Iraqi sky after the sandstorms. Reconnaissance planes and bomb damage assessment teams could see the full impact

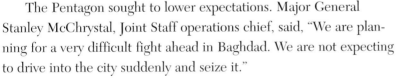

Ground crews load a sixty-six-ton M1 Abrams tank onto a C-17 Globemaster III aircraft. Tanks were airlifted into northern and western Iraq to provide heavy support for Special Operations Forces and the 173rd Airborne Brigade.

of the weeks-long bombing campaign. It was far more devastating than they had anticipated.

The Republican Guard units were decimated. Those who weren't killed had disappeared. The scope of the destruction was apparent in a remark by General Myers, speaking not only of the attacks on the Republican Guard units but of the entire bombing and artillery campaign. He claimed that of the eight hundred tanks Iraq had at the beginning of the war, all but nineteen had been destroyed. But what of the casualty toll among Iraqi troops?

"One of the yet-to-be-told stories of the war is the extent of the Iraqi war dead," Bill Wheatley said. "The U.S. hasn't said much about Iraqi casualties and the Iraqis have given estimates only of civilian deaths. Given the amount of ordnance that has been dropped on the Iraqi armies, the total of dead and wounded must be substantial. But how many?"

Wheatley's question went unanswered. At no time did Iraqi or Central Command officials offer an estimate of how many Iraqi troops were killed in the entire war. As coalition forces were closing in on Baghdad, the focus was not on casualties but on the last phase of the campaign.

At Camp Lejeune, North Carolina, President Bush said, "A vise is closing on the regime. Our destination is Baghdad. What we have begun, we will finish."

"For the senior leadership, there is no way out," said Defense Secretary Rumsfeld. "Their fate has been sealed by their actions."

But on Iraqi TV, a statement attributed to Saddam Hussein urged the Iraqi people to "fight them with your hands."

Under normal circumstances, the drive along Iraq's modern highway from Basra to Baghdad takes a few hours.

Hands, maybe, but it would not be with chemical weapons. Despite the weeks and months of preparation and concern, and despite one of the main justifications for preemptive war offered by the U.S. and British governments, no chemical, biological, or nuclear material was used—or found—during the course of the war. Nor did U.S. troops find a single Scud missile, a prime suspect for delivery of WMD. This would continue to be the state of affairs long after the collapse of Saddam Hussein's regime. NBC analyst David Kay discussed the implications with Tom Brokaw.

161

As the war progressed, the initial torrent of Iraqi POWs slowed to a trickle. While thousands were captured around Basra, only handfuls were taken as the Army and Marines moved north. Iraqi soldiers shed their uniforms and blended back into the civilian population, and many U.S. units faced only Fedayeen and paramilitary fighters, many of whom did not wear uniforms.

"This war was justified in large part because of the threat of Saddam Hussein's weapons of mass destruction and the danger that he might pass them to others," he said. "We've got to find those weapons and we've got to find them in a way that is absolutely, convincingly transparent to the rest of the world that we didn't plant the evidence." (On June 11, 2003, David Kay was appointed special U.S. adviser in charge of the overall search for weapons of mass destruction in Iraq.)

With no WMD and with Iraqi forces melting away, coalition troops and embedded reporters did not encounter what they expected. Everywhere, Chip Reid saw destroyed armor and green uniforms abandoned along the road. Reid recalls that the questions in everybody's mind were, "Where did they go? Did they just blend back into society, or did they fall back into Baghdad where they're going to hit us really hard when we get there?"

For the moment, however, the troops were meeting Iraqi civilians, not soldiers. The receptions ranged from angry to noncommittal to joyous. In Nasiriyah, Marine Lance Corporal Alex Rivera jumped on the hood of a Humvee, and a group of kids crowded around. "I got kind of crazy, and they looked kind of sad and down," Rivera remembered thinking. "So I wanted to liven them up a little bit." He succeeded.

Marine Lance Corporal Alex Rivera leads Iraqi children in a rap song in Nasiriyah.

Rivera: "Ready?"
Kids: "Ready."
Rivera: "We ready."
Kids: "We ready."
Rivera: "Come on, you all."
Kids: "Come on, you all."
Rivera: "We be ready."
Kids: "We be ready."

An Iraqi man handed a letter to a Marine who passed it on to Chip Reid.

"To whome save us, save our country, save the world from the devil . . .

"My pen can't write evry thing—but only I want to say to you Thank you, Thank you, Thank you . . .

"Please, I want from you to send this letter to any family who lose here sone, here daughter in this battle in the way of peace say to them we will not forget them. We will remember them evry time. I am Islamic man, from my country say again Thank you. I hope you go to your home taking with you our love making friendship."

As the troops had their encounters with Iraqi civilians and coalition forces were poised to invade Baghdad, there were developments of a different sort.

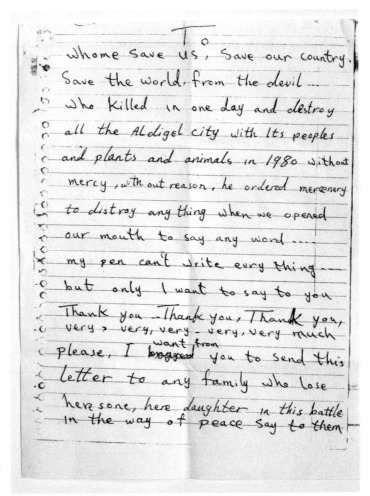

163

On April 4, forty-six-year-old Michael Kelly became the first American journalist to die in the war. Kelly, a *Washington Post* columnist and *Atlantic Monthly* editor, was embedded with the 3rd Infantry Division. He died when his Humvee flipped over near the airport west of Baghdad.

On the same day, not far from the airport, David Bloom delivered what proved to be his last report for NBC News:

"The job of the force we're with is to guard a bridge, a critical crossing over the Euphrates River. So critical that the Iraqis keep trying to take back the bridge with disastrous results. The charred remains of Iraqi tanks litter the main roadway. Destroyed Iraqi armored personnel carriers smolder in tall grass near the riverbanks. Pickup trucks, filled with Iraqi soldiers, carried them only to their graves."

Bloom never got to Baghdad. Two days later, he suffered a pulmonary embolism and died. Producer Paul Nassar recalls that Bloom had just emerged from the Bloommobile, smiling to himself after listening to his telephone messages. Nassar looked away for a moment, heard a soldier shout, and turned to see Bloom collapsed on the sand.

Bloom's body was flown back to Kuwait City, where Heather Allan, NBC's Kuwait City bureau chief, was waiting. Soon after, Kerry Sanders called Allan to ask about the arrival. She told him that the plane carried many others who had died in Iraq. Then she added, "There were so many bodies, and every one of them was somebody's David Bloom."

The day after Bloom's death, retired General Montgomery Meigs reflected on the correspondent's legacy in a note to the NBC News staff. "David led by who he was, that ball of energy blazing across the sky that captures one's imagination of worlds to be pursued and found."

The death of David Bloom certainly touched millions of Americans who had been enthralled by his reporting. Viewers sent tens of thousands of e-mail messages to NBC News, many with poignant stories of what Bloom's reporting had meant to them personally.

Some days later, in his eulogy at St. Patrick's Cathedral, Tom Brokaw expressed the collective feelings of all of David's colleagues, shaken by the loss of a familiar presence who somehow came to represent something larger than a single individual: "We are one family in our grief, and our grief is so great because the hole is so large."

AMERICA AT HOME

FOR MANY, A REAL WAR. Whether it was laying family members to rest, demonstrating in the streets, wishing family and friends good luck and welcome home, or giving blood for the cause, Americans all showed their patriotism and passion. ▦

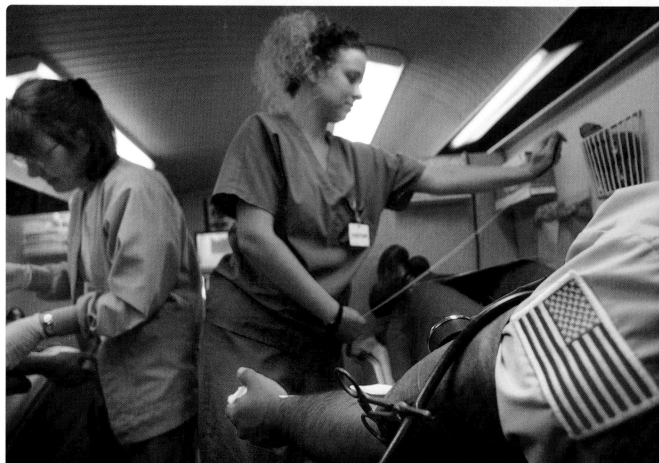

CHAPTER 10

BAGHDAD

Twenty-four hours after David Bloom's death, almost to the minute, cameraman Craig White was standing beneath a south Baghdad overpass called Curly. It was one of three strategically important intersections that U.S. forces had designated Objectives Curly, Larry, and Moe.

Producer Paul Nassar had stayed behind with Bloom's body for the trip back to Kuwait. White decided to press on to Baghdad because, as he put it, it's what David would have wanted. Now he was with a medical team that accompanied about eighty soldiers of the 3rd Infantry Division whose objective was to take the intersection. According to an informal Army evaluation of what happened there, Curly "was defended with a level of fanaticism unknown to us since the banzai charges of the Japanese in the Pacific." White said, "It was modern warfare. Things really blowing up large."

Left: Army Staff Sergeant Joe Todd of TF 3-15 Infantry, photographed during the fighting at Objective Curly on April 7. *Below:* A TF 3-15 Infantry Humvee speeds past abandoned and destroyed Iraqi equipment at Engagement Area Hanna south of Baghdad on April 5.

Burning U.S. Special Forces vehicles under a highway overpass at Objective Curly.

The trouble began when two Iraqi T-72 tanks pulled within fifty meters of a platoon leader, who quickly jumped into a nearby shallow ditch. With heavy fire passing inches over his head, he screamed to his senior noncommissioned officer, a sergeant, to get the rest of the platoon to safety. The sergeant refused. Instead, he drove into the open, waving his arms to attract the attention of the men in the Iraqi tanks. This allowed the platoon leader to scramble out of the ditch to safety, unhurt except for temporary deafness caused by the explosions all around him. Moments later, a U.S. M1 tank burst into the fight and within seconds destroyed the two Iraqi tanks.

The Army report says that most of the enemy forces were Syrians intent on fighting to the death. They attacked repeatedly for the next twelve to fourteen hours. Craig White's camera kept rolling. "About six hours in, it didn't look good," he recalled later. "I thought we were going to be overrun. They started hitting vehicles all around us."

A U.S. truck convoy arrived with ammunition and fuel. Enemy troops fired rocket-propelled grenades, igniting part of the convoy and killing two Americans instantly. The dead and wounded on both sides were brought to the medical unit, where White was amazed by what he saw. "It was very strange to me that American soldiers were treating Syrian wounded as they treated American wounded, side by side."

Command Sergeant Major Robert "Bob" Gallagher and Captain Erik Schobitz, M.D., TF 3-15 battalion surgeon, during the fighting at Objective Curly on April 7.

171

Above: An Army sergeant works to move a truck away from burning ammunition during the battle at Objective Curly on April 7. *Right:* Command Sergeant Major Bob Gallagher continues to fight as his leg is bandaged during the battle for Objective Curly.

White said he saw medics running to places under fire to retrieve wounded Syrians. He saw Sergeant Joe Todd prevent a huge explosion by jumping into an ammunition truck and moving it away from an adjacent burning vehicle. He saw Sergeant Bob Gallagher standing and firing his rifle at enemy troops while medics were removing shrapnel from his leg. And he saw Private Second Class Christopher Nauman firing his weapon while lying on a stretcher being treated for a leg wound.

"It was an amazing sight," Craig White remembers. "The ammo trucks got hit. The fuel trucks got hit. The chaplain of our unit

picked up an M16 and started firing. It came down to me giving ammo to people, which is something I never thought I'd have to do."

White got out after seven hours. It wasn't until the next day that U.S. forces finally took Objective Curly, while other 3rd ID soldiers took Larry and Moe. Three days later, White and his pictures were shown on *Nightly News.* In his report, White said, "In another war, it could have been a mountain with a number or a beach with no name. Were it not for these pictures, no one would remember this. I'll never forget it."

Soldiers from Company B, TF 3-15 Infantry take cover in an Iraqi trench underneath the highway at Objective Curly on April 7.

ONE UNIT'S JOURNEY
TF 3-15 INFANTRY

Reaches Obj. Lyons (Saddam International Airport)
4/4

Baghdad

Final attack position west of Euphrates at Obj. Peach
4/3

4/9 TF 3-15 reaches downtown Baghdad

After transiting Karbala gap waits for darkness to cross Euphrates River
4/2

4/7 Three-day fight to seize Objs. Larry, Moe, and Curly

Karbala

4/6 Fighting rages at Obj. Grady (Iskandariyah airfield)

Stalled at TAA Spartan 4 for five days **3/24**

4/5 Fighting continues at main Euphrates bridgehead (Engagement Area Hanna)

Republican Guard Medina division assessed as destroyed, and battalion receives change of mission to secure Euphrates crossings. Intense fighting continues at Euphrates River crossings until April 6.

Najaf

The fight to protect the 2nd Brigade's lines of communication in support of the attack into Baghdad culminates at three highway interchange objectives. At Objective Moe, eight hours of sustained combat results in more than sixty Iraqi vehicles destroyed with some two hundred dead. Buses of uniformed Special Republican Guardsmen are destroyed. At Objective Larry, more than sixty vehicles are destroyed; some three hundred Iraqi infantry are killed. At Objective Curly, two U.S. soldiers are killed and nine are seriously wounded in action.

3/23 Seizure and clearing of Obj. Rams

The task force suffers through a three-day sandstorm as the Iraqis attempt to counterattack from the west and are destroyed by air strikes. Conducts reconnaissance of the Karbala gap. On March 30, begins three days of operations against Iraqi defenders south and west of Karbala.

Samawah

3/22 Linkup at Obj. Martin at 17:15

After driving with only a short refueling in the desert, battalion task forces link up at Objective Martin south of Samawah.

Excerpt of hand-drawn map kept by Craig White, NBC cameraman, embedded with 3-15 Infantry.

Nasiriyah

IRAQ

Task Force 3-15 Infantry, 2nd Brigade Combat Team, 3rd Infantry Division (Mechanized) executed OPLAN CHINA COBRA II, fighting from western Kuwait to Saddam International Airport and downtown Baghdad. With 836 assigned soldiers and the attached B Company, 4th Battalion, 64th Armor, and A Company, 10th Engineer Battalion, Task Force China sees some of the war's most intense fighting and defeats the last Iraqi defenders in south Baghdad.

3/20 TF Heavy Metal crosses border at 21:20

KUWAIT

CROSSINGS

THE WATER FRONT Central Iraq is defined by its great rivers, the Euphrates and the Tigris, which wind their way through the Mesopotamian valley. Most Army and Marine units had to cross not one but two rivers on their way to Baghdad. *Top:* To cross the Euphrates River, 3rd ID scouts and engineers used inflatable boats and, *bottom,* went into the water to cut wires rigged to explosives attached to river crossings.

Top: Supply vehicles from the 3rd ID travel across the Euphrates River on a pontoon bridge built by engineers. *Bottom:* Marines build a floating bridge to get across the Diyala River east of Baghdad.

Top: A view of Baghdad from a Marine helicopter over Sadr City (previously Saddam City), one of Baghdad's poorest districts. *Above:* MSNBC correspondent Bob Arnot with the 1st Marine Division east of Baghdad. Arnot traveled with producer Jim Bruton.

The three overpasses were not the only hot spots in Baghdad. In fact, fighting had erupted elsewhere before the battles of Moe, Larry, and Curly were under way. The 1st Marine Division approached Baghdad up Highway 6 from the southeast, an area defended by remnants of the Republican Guards' al-Nida division. The Iraqi forces, aided by jihad warriors from other nations, attacked with mortar fire, rocket-propelled grenades, and small arms ambushes.

MSNBC correspondent Bob Arnot had been embedded with the Marines since the beginning of the war and was with them as they approached the Diyala River, where they searched for crossing points. But bridges had already been disabled or were suspected of being rigged with explosives. The Marines decided to fabricate their own span by laying an expeditionary bridge across the Diyala. Others came up with a simpler solution. Arnot saw a Marine take off his gear, jump into the river, swim across, swim back, and pronounce the river fit to be

ONE UNIT'S JOURNEY
3/5 MARINES

4/8 Crosses Diyala River and proceeds to northeast Baghdad

Baghdad

4/6 Camps at division objective east of the Diyala River

Eight hours of close combat along Highway 6.

Unit moves across Diyala River to consolidate north of Baghdad in the vicinity of Highway 5 before conducting a linkup with the 3rd Infantry Division on April 9, isolating the capital from the north.

4/4 Battles east of Salman Pak

RCT 5 faces its most significant conventional battle in Aziziyah against T-55 and T-62 tanks, mechanized vehicles, artillery, and mortars from the Republican Guard units.

4/3 Battles to clear forces in Aziziyah

Hillah

3/27 Regiment attacks Hantush airstrip but then withdraws for pause

4/2 Crosses Tigris River at Numaniyah

The unit's main effort with 2nd Tank Battalion and 1st Light Armored Reconnaissance Battalion to cross the Tigris River. Faces a reinforced Iraqi battalion; numerous tanks and vehicles hit with RPG and small-arms fire.

Diwaniyah

3/24 Leads RCT-5 to consolidate east of Diwaniyah

3/5 Marines engage company-sized Fedayeen and irregular forces, experiences intense sandstorm and golf ball–sized hailstones.

Excerpt of hand-drawn map kept by Chip Reid, NBC embed with 3/5 Marines.

IRAQ

3/23 Crosses Euphrates River at 12:30

Nasiriyah

Regimental Combat Team 5 (RCT 5) crosses into Iraq as the 1st Marine Division's main effort with 7,503 Marines, sailors, and U.S. and British soldiers supported by over two thousand vehicles, including tanks and light armored vehicles.

3/23 Departs at 05:30

The 3rd Battalion, 5th Marines (3/5 Marines) of Regimental Combat Team 5 moved over one thousand kilometers through April 20, 2002. The Regiment spent eighteen days in MOPP 1 or 2 (chemical suits). Combat losses included twelve killed in action and 126 wounded.

3/21 Seizes Gas Oil Separation Plants 1 and 2

Basra

3/20 Departs TAA in Kuwait at 16:30

KUWAIT

3rd ID soldiers take cover outside the VIP terminal at Saddam International Airport. Though U.S. forces reached the airport runways on the night of April 3, they continued to battle with the last Iraqi defenders for a week.

crossed. So the Marines got into their amphibious assault vehicles and launched an invasion of Baghdad, hundreds of miles from the nearest coastline. Soon after, the Marines captured the Rasheed military airfield, three miles east of the city center.

An even bigger prize lay to the west—Baghdad's main airport, Saddam International. The 3rd ID swept into the airport, where it was soon joined by troops from the 101st Airborne. Over the next several days, the 101st reported killing several hundred Iraqi troops while securing the airport. As seven thousand U.S. troops were establishing a base of operations there, Iraqi Information Minister al-Sahaf announced, "We slaughtered them in the airport. They are out of Saddam International Airport."

Between the airports, all across southern Baghdad, Marines engaged in close-quarter fighting with pro-Saddam volunteers from

Syria, Jordan, Egypt, and Sudan. At the same time, an armored battalion of the 3rd ID sent a clear message to Iraqi citizens and soldiers by making its first so-called thunder run into downtown Baghdad from Objectives Moe, Larry, and Curly. The unit was fired on from rooftops and ditches along the sides of the highway, but it reached the center of the city. Then it turned west and headed toward the airport. The point was made: We have arrived.

While the battle for Baghdad unfolded, there were developments in southern Iraq as British forces entered and finally took control of most of Basra, Iraq's second city. It had taken two weeks of fighting to accomplish. In northern Iraq, despite steady progress by coalition forces, there was another deadly mistake—another friendly fire incident. U.S. aircraft attacked a convoy of U.S. Special Operations troops and Kurdish fighters, killing eighteen Kurds. A BBC crew was there, and its translator was also killed.

NBC anchor Brian Williams made it to Saddam International on April 9. Around the periphery of the sprawling complex were three Saddam Hussein palaces, all complete with intricate moats and bridges.

181

Right: The governorate headquarters building in Basra. On April 6, British forces moved into Basra, destroying Ba'ath Party headquarters and battling the last paramilitary fighters, losing three soldiers. The 3rd Battalion Parachute Regiment later cleared the city's old quarter on foot, the streets too congested for armored vehicles. *Above:* Moments after the northern Iraq friendly fire attack in which he was wounded, BBC correspondent John Simpson broadcast live by satellite telephone. A BBC cameraman received minor injuries but continued to film with his blood dripping on the lens.

NBC's Tom Aspell was not far away and soon after reported on what had occurred in front of the BBC camera. "The cameraman must have been carrying his camera on his lap and switched it on the moment the bomb hit. The first thing you see is a drop of blood falling on the lens and you realize the cameraman had been hit somewhere, enough to splash blood." But he kept the camera rolling, permitting BBC correspondent John Simpson, who was slightly injured, to give a dramatic first-person account of the havoc.

The details of an earlier incident of mayhem finally began to emerge. Central Command identified eight dead U.S. soldiers from the 507th Maintenance Company that had made a wrong turn in Nasiriyah back on March 23. The bodies had been located at the hospital where Jessica Lynch was found. Among the dead was twenty-three-year-old Private First Class Lori Piestewa of Tuba City, Arizona. It would not be until eight days after the Centcom announcement that the fate of the other missing soldiers would emerge. Seven of them were found in northern Iraq, alive and in relatively good condition. They were flown to Kuwait.

In Baghdad, Iraqi officials and residents watched as their situation unraveled. On April 7, several developments clearly showed that the end was near. Elements of the 3rd ID entered downtown for good, seizing the Republican and Sijood presidential palaces. At the same time, other U.S. soldiers toppled a statue of Saddam Hussein at the parade grounds where he often reviewed his troops. In an echo of the first night of the war, a B-1B bomber dropped four precision-guided two-thousand-pound bombs on a suspected meeting of Iraqi officials, possibly including Saddam Hussein, in the Mansour section of the capital.

Amid these events, Information Minister Mohammed al-Sahaf—Baghdad Bob—stood on a downtown street and made another announcement that would provide more fodder for late-night comedians back in the States. "The infidels are committing suicide by the hundreds on the gates of Baghdad," he said. "There is no presence of the American columns in the city of Baghdad at all. We besieged them, and we killed most of them. The soldiers of Saddam Hussein have given them a lesson they will never forget."

During the battle for Baghdad, Bob Arnot reached a hospital where Iraqi doctors were operating on a little girl who had shrapnel in her small intestines and liver. Arnot, a doctor himself, asked one of the surgeons if the girl would live. "She's the future of Iraq," the doctor said. "Of course she's going to live."

Left: Coalition personnel worked hard treating Iraqi wounded on the battlefield, both civilians and military. *Above:* Billboard-sized pictures of Saddam Hussein were in every village, at every crossing, and in front of every government building and school throughout the country.

OPULENCE

SQUANDERED IRAQI TREASURE. In Baghdad alone, Saddam Hussein built seven palaces for himself and his family. Soldiers found ornate wreckage in the wake of coalition attacks by precision-guided weapons. *Next page, clockwise from top:* The red phone by the indoor pool at Saddam's main palace in Tikrit. A simple note left by a soldier in a senior Ba'ath Party official's Baghdad home. A stack of gold-plated Kalashnikov rifles seized from a house belonging to Saddam's son Uday. *Following page:* An Iraqi dinar goes up in smoke as U.S. forces discover hundreds of millions of dollars and other valuables stored in Iraqi palaces and hideaways. ▨

CHAPTER 11

REGIME CHANGE

By April 8, Saddam's regime had been pushed from its seat of power, the Republican Guards had been destroyed, and coalition forces were making inroads throughout Baghdad, yet danger and confusion reigned all over the capital. The 3rd Infantry Division already occupied parts of downtown Baghdad, and Marine units were pressing in from the eastern suburbs. Caught between them were remnants of Ba'ath Party militias, palace guards, Army loyalists, and Fedayeen irregulars, all of them fighting not because of a carefully planned defense of the city, but because coalition forces were near and getting nearer.

Left: Marines advance through a wall of smoke on Uday Hussein's Fedayeen headquarters in northeast Baghdad. *Below:* 3/7 Marines fought house to house in north and eastern Baghdad against Fedayeen fighters.

Top: A Bradley Fighting Vehicle of Task Force 2-69 Armor, 3rd ID, fires on Iraqi forces in northern Baghdad. Even with the disappearance of the Iraqi government, pockets of fighting continued. *Below:* Working from NBC News Studio 3C in New York, Tom Brokaw kept the nation up to date with all the latest developments.

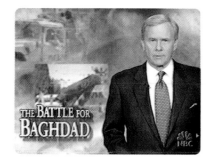

Iraqi snipers fired from a number of government buildings, including the high-rise Planning Ministry and the office of the prime minister. The difficulty of pinpointing the snipers' whereabouts led to more unintended deaths. As a U.S. tank crossed the Jumhuriyah bridge, sniper fire came from the north bank of the Tigris River. That was the general direction of the Palestine Hotel, where many foreign journalists were staying. The tank returned fire, as it had been doing all day, and the shell hit the hotel, killing a Spanish network cameraman and a Ukrainian cameraman who worked for Reuters.

Centcom and the Pentagon defended the action, saying that the tank responded to sniper fire coming from the hotel. A number of foreign journalists inside the Palestine, however, reported that they heard no sniper fire coming from the building. On the same day, a U.S. air strike hit another building that housed Arab media, killing a Jordanian correspondent who worked for al-Jazeera, the most popular news network in the Arab world.

Iraq TV went off the air on April 8, after announcing what would prove to be the government's final casualty toll. The dispatch reported

In downtown Baghdad, U.S. tanks and infantry continued to fight snipers and loyalists hiding in government buildings. In one of the most widely disputed incidents of the war, a tank fired on the Palestine Hotel, killing two journalists.

that 1,252 Iraq civilians had been killed and 5,103 wounded. There was no further clarification of the toll from any Iraqi source, so confusion reigned on this issue as well. Over the next two months, three American news organizations estimated death tolls ranging from 1,700 to 3,240 civilians. All three studies acknowledged that they did not, and could not, account for the casualties that never reached a hospital. The true toll will never be known.

With coalition troops and armor pushing through the streets of Baghdad, Information Minister Mohammed Saeed al-Sahaf made his last public statement. "We are in control," he said. "They are in a state of hysteria."

In northern Iraq, there was further confirmation of what had become increasingly obvious: There would be no major resistance to U.S. troops and their Kurdish allies. Special Operations Forces and Kurdish Peshmerga soldiers took partial control of Kirkuk, often described as the Kurds' Jerusalem. Mosul, and later Tikrit, Saddam Hussein's hometown, also offered little resistance to coalition forces. The reason was simple and brutal: Since the beginning of the war,

Top: Kurdish fighters wait to enter the city of Mosul, which fell after a cease-fire agreement was brokered with the Iraqi regular army's 5th Corps. *Above:* NBC correspondent Tom Aspell reports from northern Iraq.

Iraqi forces in the north had been decimated by nonstop bombing, most of it unseen by television cameras. One Kurdish official told NBC's Tom Aspell, "Thank you to the United States, thank you to the United Kingdom, thank you for all who stood behind us in our hour of need."

Aspell witnessed the Kurds joyously greeting the liberation of Kirkuk. "The fall of Kirkuk was largely bloodless," he reported. "By midday, crowds were in the streets celebrating the end of Saddam Hussein's rule here, defacing his portraits, pulling his statues down. The only shooting in Kirkuk now is in celebration."

In Baghdad on the same day, the 3rd Infantry Division finished clearing Highway 8 linking the city with the now-renamed Baghdad International Airport. Marine and Infantry units moved in concert to cut off any Iraqi retreat to the north. As they moved into the heart of Baghdad, it was evident, despite snipers and holdouts, that the city was now theirs. At the Palestine Hotel, journalists noticed that their "minders"—the Iraqis assigned to escort them on their assignments and monitor everything they did and everyone they spoke to—did not show up for work.

Outside the hotel, several hundred people gathered in Firdos circle around a huge statue of Saddam Hussein. Amid cheers and laughter, U.S. Marines helped Iraqis drape cables around the statue in order to pull it down. At one point a corporal, swept up in the moment, put an American flag over the statue's head. But moments later the commander on the ground, mindful of an earlier Pentagon directive, ordered it removed. So the red, white, and blue came down and the red, green, and black of the Iraqi flag replaced it. Correspondent Jim Miklaszewski explained why: "Orders had gone out not to make a public display of the flag, fearing it would appear that the U.S. had come to conquer Iraq."

Anchors Katie Couric and Tom Brokaw on *Today* the morning of April 9. U.S. Marines reached downtown Baghdad and helped crowds topple a giant statue of Saddam Hussein in Firdos circle just outside the Palestine Hotel.

Once the flag was removed, the process continued, with an M88 tank recovery vehicle yanking on the cables. But the Saddam statue, like Saddam himself, did not fall quickly or easily. First, it toppled ninety degrees and stopped parallel to the ground, still hanging from its pedestal. Then, after more cable placement and renewed tugging, it finally tumbled all the way to the ground while the crowd cheered.

As all this unfolded in Baghdad, NBC in New York was riveted. On *Today*, Tom Brokaw commented that Saddam "has been toppled from his pedestal, head down, no dignity, no power, no standing." Brokaw remembers that as he watched, he wondered where Saddam and his family were at the moment his likeness crashed to the ground. And he flashed back to 1989, when statues and Communist regimes were toppling all across eastern Europe. Katie Couric said, "Tom, just as you witnessed at the Berlin Wall, everybody grabbing a chunk when it fell, I'm sure everyone right now is trying to get a piece of Saddam."

The *Today* control room approached pandemonium. Producers bellowed at the director. The director scanned the monitors and roared for this or that live feed, according to which one offered the best view. Everyone knew that this was the emblematic moment of the war, the

STATUES

FALLEN SYMBOLS. He was everywhere, and then he was gone. Statues and billboards of Saddam Hussein were ubiquitous in Iraq, and their elimination became one of the first acts that Iraqis could participate in as the regime fell. ▦

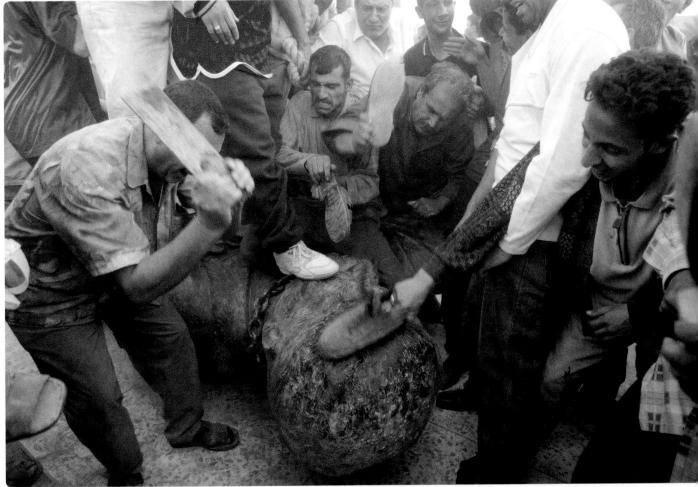

image that everybody would remember. Moments later, after Iraqis with sticks and hammers had attacked the statue's head, it was time for a videotape replay of what had just happened. Senior producer Bob Epstein, connected by intercom to the tape-editing area, barked through his microphone: "Gimme smashing head! I need smashing head!"

Producing or watching television at that moment, it could almost seem as if all Baghdad, all Iraq, were here in this one location, and all of the country's problems and possibilities were expressed in this one event. Of course, it was not so. Just blocks away and at various places around the city, firefights and ambushes continued, as they were to continue in the weeks and months ahead. Brian Williams, who had made his way to Baghdad from Kuwait, observed that while people around the world might be transfixed by the image and symbolism of a fallen statue, "the truth on the ground was markedly different. It was Fort Apache. It was open gunfights with the coalition." Reporting from Baghdad, illuminated by two flashlights because the power had been knocked out, Williams said, "Depending on where you are, it sure feels and sounds and looks like a hot zone."

Widespread looting broke out all over the city and, for that matter, all over the country. Williams said that in several places in downtown Baghdad, every able-bodied adult he saw was stealing something. Dana Lewis witnessed one of Saddam's palaces being stripped clean.

Right: Downtown, in the elbow of the Tigris River, dozens of palaces, VIP homes, ministries, barracks, and offices needed to be cleared and secured. *Opposite, top:* The festival and parade grounds at the foot of Zawra Park adjacent to the elbow. The Hands of Victory monument towers 150 feet above the parade ground, shaped from Iran-Iraq war materials. The fists and arms that hold the swords are modeled after Saddam Hussein's own. *Opposite, bottom:* NBC anchor Brian Williams at the parade grounds on April 9.

SPECIAL OPERATIONS AND KURDISH TROOPS TAKE PARTIAL CONTROL OF KIRKUK | CEASE-FIRE AGREEMENT

"People were taking chandeliers, door frames, doors, window frames, smashed plates," he said. "Why would anybody take smashed plates?" Watching it unfold, Lewis speculated that the palaces represented great symbols of authority and repression to the people who were now grabbing everything they could. Doing so, Lewis thought, "somehow made them cleansed, somehow made them feel that they were paying Saddam back."

On the day that the looting became wide-spread, Chip Reid encountered Major General James N. Mattis, commander of the 1st Marine Division. Reid asked the general if the city was in chaos. Mattis replied, "If a million smiling faces and a handful of thugs stealing furniture from a government building is chaos, then we've got chaos. But

Right: The old city near the Central Bank building, in background. *Below:* As downtown Baghdad was secured, fighting continued on the outskirts of the city.

Iraqi Ambassador to the United Nations Mohammed al-Douri speaks with reporters after leaving his residence in New York on April 9.

by any other definition, we do not have chaos." In another indication of trouble to come, however, a suicide bomber blew himself up in downtown Baghdad, wounding four U.S. Marines, adding to the total of more than six hundred coalition troops wounded or killed.

Nevertheless, President Bush and Prime Minister Blair felt confident enough to address the Iraqi people on April 10, four days before the Pentagon would officially declare "major combat engagements" to be over. The speeches were broadcast with Arabic subtitles from a C-130 Hercules aircraft called *Compass Call*.

Bush: "At this moment, the regime of Saddam Hussein is being removed from power, and a long era of fear and cruelty is ending."

Blair: "Saddam Hussein's regime is collapsing; the years of brutality, oppression, and fear are coming to an end."

But the most succinct comment about the true state of affairs had actually come the day before from, ironically enough, an Iraqi official. Mohammed al-Douri, Iraq's U.N. ambassador and the only high-ranking member of the regime who had not yet dropped from sight, was besieged by reporters outside his New York City residence. Al-Douri expressed hope that Iraqis would soon be able to live in peace. "The game," he said, "is over."

LOOTING

PAYBACK. Looters first targeted palaces and government buildings, but the wild spree soon spread to hospitals, banks, and museums. On April 12, American forces agreed to team up with Iraqi police to stem the widespread looting. ▮

CHAPTER 12

FOG OF PEACE

Most schoolchildren are taught that the land now called Iraq was once the cradle of civilization, with names like Mesopotamia, Assyria, Babylonia, and Sumer. In the eighth century, Arab geographers began using the term "El Iraq," which means "the shore of a great river along its length, as well as the grazing land surrounding it." This referred to the immense fertile plain between the Tigris and Euphrates Rivers.

Hundreds of years later, the area became part of the Ottoman Empire and remained so until the empire's collapse in World War I. At war's end, France and Britain carved up the empire and Iraq,

Some soldiers were greeted at home by their families, while the majority of U.S. forces remained in Iraq. *Left:* Captain Fred Atwater hugs his wife, Genee, and his children, Freddy and Julia. *Below:* Marines of 1st Battalion, 5th Marines, patrol the streets of northern Baghdad.

The messages in Iraq were mixed. It was liberation from Saddam Hussein, but in some areas, such as in the Fallujah corridor to the west of the capital, the sentiment was decidedly anti-American.

comprising the regions of Baghdad, Basra, and Mosul, came under British authority.

The following decades brought independence, monarchy, military coups, and authoritarian government. In 1979, Saddam Hussein took power and kept it until the war that the United States named Operation Iraqi Freedom removed him, bringing Iraq-U.S. relations full circle. Through most of the 1980s, the United States had been an ally in Iraq's war with Iran and remained so even after Saddam used

chemical weapons against Iranian forces and, later, against the Kurds of northern Iraq. But then Saddam invaded Kuwait and the United States led a large coalition to oust the Iraqis in the Gulf War of 1991.

After the Gulf War came sanctions and the U.N. inspectors' search for weapons of mass destruction. The inspectors left in 1998 but returned in 2002 as part of an effort to force Saddam to comply with a decade of U.N. Security Council resolutions. An increasingly rancorous debate ensued, with the United States, Great Britain, and Spain advocating a more confrontational policy, while Russia, France, Germany, and China urged more time for the inspectors to continue their search. This debate intensified from the summer of 2002 until March 19, 2003, the night the bombs started falling.

The following twenty-two days of fighting, despite much public discourse about the adequacy of the coalition's war plan, demonstrated the agility, power, and dominance of the U.S. military. In just over three weeks of war, coalition forces swept across Iraq and achieved one of the stated goals of the war, toppling Saddam Hussein and his

Above: Ceremonial missiles for parade use found in a hangar at Saddam International Airport. Even before the shooting stopped, Special Operations Forces and a joint Defense Department–intelligence community special task force began searching for weapons of mass destruction. *Next page:* Young Iraqis race with tanks on their bikes as British troops secure the town of Medina in southern Iraq.

regime. As Iraqi troops surrendered, Centcom official Captain Frank Thorp said, "They have made the very wise choice of living for the future of Iraq instead of dying for this Iraqi regime."

For the U.S. military, the lessons of Operation Iraqi Freedom will undoubtedly help shape the armed forces of the future. The implications, of course, are enormous—for the way wars are waged, for the budgetary battles that lie ahead, and for the manner in which the United States relates to the rest of the world, both militarily and diplomatically. The superiority of the U.S. military on the ground and in the air was magnified by all types of information technology—intelligence, satellite imaging, communications, and damage assessment, to name just a few.

As the war unfolded, a hotly debated military question emerged: Were there enough boots on the ground? By favoring mobility and improvisation over a larger, more traditional force, was the military helping or hurting its mission? As things worked out, several

An Iraqi family buries its dead. Surveys of Iraqi hospitals conducted by three separate news organizations in May and June concluded that as many as 3,240 civilians died and more than 8,000 were injured in the war.

212

unanticipated developments complicated this question. The Iraqi Fedayeen paramilitaries launched their ambushes, the sandstorms struck, and the coalition push to Baghdad paused. But the air campaign did not stop; strikes continued all over Iraq, especially south of Baghdad where Republican Guard divisions were poised to engage coalition forces heading north toward the capital. The pause on the ground gave the air campaign more time to inflict damage—in military lingo, the word is "attrit"—on the Iraqi forces lying in wait.

All military analysts agree that, with or without the extra time, the eventual outcome of the war was clear: Even at full strength, Iraqi forces were no match for the Americans. But had U.S. forces reached those Republican Guard units sooner, before they were virtually

Saddam Hussein used a network of underground bunkers and tunnels. Here, 3rd ID soldiers investigate the labyrinth of tunnels discovered underneath Saddam International Airport. Many of the bunkers were flooded or had been burned. U.S. investigators suspected that many had been intentionally sabotaged.

General Tommy Franks visits with troops at the renamed
Baghdad International Airport. Franks's C-130 transport
landed on a taxiway instead of a runway, which was still
obstructed by sixty-foot-wide craters caused by U.S. bombing. Later, Franks met with his commanders at the new U.S.
headquarters, Saddam Hussein's Abu Ghraib North Palace
east of the airport.

JUBILATION

LIBERATORS. *Clockwise from top left:* Samantha Sheppard of Plymouth, England, 2nd Light Tank Regiment, smiles as she receives a flower during a patrol on the streets of Basra. An Iraqi girl holds a homemade U.S. flag as an American patrol passes her house in southern Iraq. Cheering crowds in Nasiriyah. An Army specialist gets a kiss of thanks from a young Iraqi boy in Baghdad. *Next page:* Locals cheer the arrival of U.S. forces in southern Iraq. ▧

destroyed, there surely would have been more fighting, and it is plausible that there could have been many more casualties on both sides.

As it turned out, the effect of the pause and the sandstorms may have worked to the coalition's advantage. The pause allowed U.S. ground units to reconsolidate before crossing the red line for the final assault on Baghdad. While punishing for troops on the ground, the sandstorms gave Iraqi generals confidence that they could exploit the weather and reinforce the Medina and Baghdad divisions on Saddam's front lines. But even as Republican Guard reserves moved in small groups under strict secrecy, U.S. sensors detected them and passed on their locations to waiting aircraft. While stiff fights would still take place locally on the ground, massed Iraqi counterattacks by heavy units never became a threat.

All these questions will be dissected in the months and years ahead by military officials and military historians. One such historian, Sir Max Hastings, has posed another question, concerning the enig-

Commanders of the 82nd Airborne meet with tribal and civic leaders of Diwaniyah, Iraq, to discuss electric, water, fuel, and police issues on April 11.

matic Saddam Hussein: "When military historians pick over the bones of this struggle," he wrote, "the issue that will puzzle them most is why Saddam Hussein accepted war with the U.S. when he possessed no plan for how to fight it."

Starting in mid-April, the clarity of the coalition's war was replaced by the fog of securing the peace. The difficulties continued to unfold long after Saddam and his top officials dropped from view. The United States was faced with two challenges. One was to restore security, help Iraq climb out of chaos, and avoid appearing like a great power that conquers and then departs, leaving the locals to clean up the mess. At the same time, the United States did not want to appear like an occupier intent on imposing its own will on the Iraqi people. Then there were questions about the other stated justifications for the war: Where were the weapons of mass destruction? Where was clear proof of a link between the Iraqi regime and terrorist organizations, specifically al-Qaeda?

There were questions of a different sort, as well. Just how did modern technology affect the public's understanding and experience of the war? Undoubtedly, the presence of embedded reporters had a

Brigadier General Vincent Brooks holds up the ace of clubs from a deck of cards prepared by the Defense Intelligence Agency bearing the pictures of the most-wanted Iraqi regime leaders.

221

In Baghdad and most cities in the south, the loss of electrical power was one of the greatest impediments to restoration of civilian services, as well as to nighttime security. The coalition had bombed electrical power distribution centers in many cities and towns throughout the south. In Baghdad, the power system mysteriously collapsed the night U.S. forces reached Saddam International Airport.

dramatic impact on the people at home who chose to read and watch closely. Experiencing this war from afar was different from earlier wars. But how? It's not as if embedding is a new concept. In World War II, for example, journalists such as Ernie Pyle were embedded, although the word "embedded" was never used. It was the same in Korea, a war that produced the first combat footage ever shown on television. In Vietnam, when television had become technologically advanced enough to show a great deal of that war, journalists were free to roam and report as they chose.

The phrase "living room war" was coined during the Vietnam era. At the time, with television's newfound capabilities, the phrase seemed apt. But film, not videotape, was the dominant medium of the day, and film had to be developed at a lab. That took time. And in that pre- and early satellite era, film had to be flown great distances before it could be seen on TV. That took time as well.

There were no such time constraints in Iraq, when many events were reported live, as they happened. The contrast was drawn sharply in a battle early in the war, in the southern town of Umm Qasr. In military terms, it was not significant. A handful of Iraqi forces holed up in a building were firing at a small number of coalition troops deployed on a nearby road. A British team from Sky TV was embedded at the scene, and the coverage was available to anyone who wanted it. It was a sunny midmorning in Iraq, the middle of the night in the United States. NBC and the other broadcast networks had already completed their war coverage and resumed normal programming. MSNBC, along with CNN and Fox News, televised the battle live.

It was unedited, uninterrupted, unanalyzed, unspun. It was not heightened reality or dramatized reality. But the tension was inescapable: Death was potentially near.

The minutes—many minutes—passed, and it became an agonizing waiting game—as much a part of war as bombs and bullets. Millions who decided to stay glued to their TV sets at home in the middle of the night shared the experience of these several dozen troops in Umm Qasr. Almost forty years after the phrase was coined, the living room

Sailors scrub down the flight deck of the USS *Harry S Truman* in the Persian Gulf on April 19.

No one doubted the enormity of the military victory. The peace, however, would prove vexing and deadly.

war became a reality. A coalition tank eventually destroyed the building, and the battle became a footnote. But what happened on TV had never happened before, and it raised the question of what would come next.

Today, it is possible to imagine a video camera attached to the underside of an aircraft capable of transmitting live, crisp, close-up shots of bombs exploding thousands of feet below, just as today a satellite photo taken from two hundred miles in space can clearly show an object just inches across. It is impossible, however, to imagine all the technology that will be invented in the future. For every new development and every new device, there will remain the same immutable issue and the same challenge for the military, the media, and the viewing public: We see it, but what does it mean?

The enduring meaning of Operation Iraqi Freedom must also await the passage of time, the nature of postwar Iraq, and unfolding events throughout the Middle East. That verdict is far off; indeed, it is a verdict that, by its very nature, can never be final.

So, then, what *can* be said of the war—that finite period between the night the bombs first fell and the moment twenty-two days later when Baghdad, Saddam, and his regime fell? Certainly, it is evident that

not many voices—pro- or anti-war—have been raised to dispute Vice President Cheney when he said, "The conclusion of the war will mark one of the most extraordinary military campaigns ever conducted."

Retired General Montgomery Meigs, an NBC News military analyst, points out that a key factor in waging a successful campaign is creative planning and "making fewer mistakes than the other guy. The rest," he adds, "is the performance of the men and women who actually fought the war." In the searing heat and grit of the Iraqi desert, the initial verdict on that was clear: They fought bravely and tenaciously and well.

No passage of time will change that.

IN MEMORIAM

On April 14, 2003, the Pentagon declared that major military operations had ended in Iraq. These are the soldiers and journalists who died in Operation Iraqi Freedom between March 21 and April 14, the period covered by this book.

SOLDIERS WHO DIED DURING COMBAT IN OPERATION IRAQI FREEDOM

MARCH 21

Marine Major Jay Thomas Aubin, 36, Waterville, Maine

Marine Captain Ryan Anthony Beaupre, 30, Bloomington, Illinois

Marine Second Lieutenant Therrel S. Childers, 30, Harrison County, Mississippi

Marine Lance Corporal Jose Gutierrez, 28, Los Angeles, California

Marine Corporal Brian Matthew Kennedy, 25, Houston, Texas

Marine Staff Sergeant Kendall Damon Waters-Bey, 29, Baltimore, Maryland

Color Sergeant John Cecil, Plymouth, England

Lance Bombardier Llewelyn Karl Evans, Llandudno, Wales

Captain Philip Stuart Guy, United Kingdom

Marine Sholto Hedenskog, United Kingdom

Sergeant Les Hehir, Poole, Dorset, England

Operator Mechanic Second Class Ian Seymour, United Kingdom

Warrant Officer Second Class Mark Stratford, United Kingdom

Major Jason Ward, United Kingdom

MARCH 22

Navy Lieutenant Thomas Mullen Adams, 27, La Mesa, California

Marine Sergeant Nicolas M. Hodson, 22, Smithville, Missouri

Marine Lance Corporal Eric J. Orlowski, 26, Buffalo, New York

Army Captain Christopher Scott Seifert, 27, Easton, Pennsylvania

Army Reserve Specialist Brandon S. Tobler, 19, Portland, Oregon

A 3rd Battalion, 15th Infantry, display of personal effects at a memorial service in Baghdad. The battalion honored David Bloom along with two soldiers who died during the war, Sergeant First Class John Marshall and Staff Sergeant Robert Stever.

Lieutenant Philip D. Green, United Kingdom
Lieutenant Antony King, Helston, England
Lieutenant Marc A. Lawrence, United Kingdom
Lieutenant Philip West, Budock Water, England
Lieutenant James Williams, Falmouth, England
Lieutenant Andrew S. Wilson, United Kingdom

MARCH 23

Army Specialist Jamaal R. Addison, 22, Roswell, Georgia
Army Sergeant Edward John Anguiano, 24, Los Fresnos, Texas
Marine Sergeant Michael E. Bitz, 31, Ventura, California
Marine Lance Corporal Brian Rory Buesing, 20, Cedar Key, Florida
Army Sergeant George Edward Buggs, 31, Barnwell, South Carolina
Marine Private First Class Tamario D. Burkett, 21, Buffalo, New York
Marine Corporal Kemaphoom A. Chanawongse, 22, Waterford, Connecticut
Marine Lance Corporal Donald John Cline, 21, Sparks, Nevada
Army First Sergeant Robert J. Dowdy, 38, Cleveland, Ohio
Army Private Ruben Estrella-Soto, 18, El Paso, Texas
Marine Lance Corporal David K. Fribley, 26, Fort Myers, Florida
Marine Corporal Jose A. Garibay, 21, Costa Mesa, California
Marine Private Jonathan L. Gifford, 30, Decatur, Illinois
Marine Corporal Jorge A. Gonzalez, 20, Los Angeles, California
Marine Private Nolen R. Hutchings, 19, Boiling Springs, South Carolina
Army Private First Class Howard Johnson II, 21, Mobile, Alabama
Marine Staff Sergeant Phillip A. Jordan, 42, Enfield, Connecticut
Army Specialist James Kiehl, 22, Comfort, Texas
Army Chief Warrant Officer Johnny Villareal Mata, 35, Pecos, Texas
Marine Lance Corporal Patrick R. Nixon, 21, Gallatin, Tennessee
Army Private First Class Lori Piestewa, 23, Tuba City, Arizona
Marine Second Lieutenant Frederick E. Pokorney Jr., 31, Tonopah, Nevada
Marine Sergeant Brendon Reiss, 23, Casper, Wyoming
Marine Corporal Randal Kent Rosacker, 21, San Diego, California
Army Private Brandon Sloan, 19, Bedford Heights, Ohio
Marine Lance Corporal Thomas J. Slocum, 22, Thornton, Colorado
Army Sergeant Donald Walters, 33, Kansas City, Missouri
Marine Lance Corporal Michael J. Williams, 31, Phoenix

Sapper Luke Allsopp, London, England,
Staff Sergeant Simon Cullingworth, Essex, England

Flight Lieutenant Kevin Barry Main, United Kingdom
Flight Lieutenant David Rhys Williams, United Kingdom

MARCH 24
Marine Lance Corporal Thomas A. Blair, 24, Broken Arrow, Oklahoma
Marine Corporal Evan James, 20, La Harpe, Illinois
Marine Sergeant Bradley S. Korthaus, 29, Davenport, Iowa
Army Specialist Gregory P. Sanders, 19, Hobart, Indiana

Sergeant Steven Mark Roberts, Bradford, England
Lance Corporal Barry Stephen, Perth, Scotland

MARCH 25
Marine Private First Class Francisco A. Martinez Flores, 21, Los Angeles, California
Navy Hospital Corpsman Third Class Michael Vann Johnson Jr., 25, Little Rock, Arkansas
Marine Staff Sergeant Donald C. May Jr., 31, Richmond, Virginia
Marine Lance Corporal Patrick T. O'Day, 20, Santa Rosa, California
Marine Corporal Robert M. Rodriguez, 21, New York, New York
Air Force Major Gregory Stone, 40, Boise, Idaho

Corporal Stephen John Allbutt, Stoke-on-Trent, England
Trooper David Jeffrey Clarke, Littleworth, England

MARCH 26
Marine Major Kevin G. Nave, 36, White Lake Township, Michigan

MARCH 27
Marine Gunnery Sergeant Joseph Menusa, 33, Tracy, California
Marine Lance Corporal Jesus A. Suarez Del Solar, 20, Escondido, California

MARCH 28
Marine Sergeant Fernando Padilla-Ramirez, 26, San Luis, Arizona
Army Sergeant Roderic A. Solomon, 32, Fayetteville, North Carolina

Lance Corporal Matty Hull, United Kingdom

MARCH 29
Marine Staff Sergeant James Cawley, 41, Layton, Utah
Army Corporal Michael Curtin, 23, Howell, New Jersey
Army Private First Class Diego Fernando Rincon, 19, Conyers, Georgia
Army Private First Class Michael Russell Creighton-Weldon, 20, Palm Bay, Florida

Marine Lance Corporal William W. White, 24, New York, New York
Army Sergeant Eugene Williams, 24, Highland, New York

MARCH 30
Marine Captain Aaron J. Contreras, 31, Sherwood, Oregon
Marine Sergeant Michael V. Lalush, 23, Troutville, Virginia
Marine Sergeant Brian McGinnis, 23, St. Georges, Delaware

Major Stephen A. Ballard, United Kingdom
Lance Corporal Shaun Andrew Brierley, United Kingdom
Royal Marine Christopher R. Maddison, United Kingdom

MARCH 31
Army Specialist William A. Jeffries, 39, Evansville, Indiana
Army Specialist Brandon Rowe, 20, Roscoe, Illinois

Staff Sergeant Chris Muir, Romsey, England

APRIL 1
Army Sergeant Jacob L. Butler, 24, Wellsville, Kansas
Marine Lance Corporal Joseph B. Maglione, 22, Lansdale, Pennsylvania

Lance Corporal Karl Shearer, United Kingdom
Lieutenant Alexander Tweedie, United Kingdom

APRIL 2
Army Captain James F. Adamouski, 29, Springfield, Virginia
Marine Lance Corporal Brian E. Anderson, 26, Durham, North Carolina
Army Specialist Mathew Boule, 22, Dracut, Massachusetts
Army Master Sergeant George A. Fernandez, 36, El Paso, Texas
Marine Private First Class Christian D. Gurtner, 19, Ohio City, Ohio
Army Chief Warrant Officer Erik A. Halvorsen, 40, Bennington, Vermont
Army Chief Warrant Officer Scott Jamar, 32, Granbury, Texas
Army Sergeant Michael Pedersen, 26, Flint, Michigan
Army Chief Warrant Officer Eric A. Smith, 42, Rochester, New York
Navy Lieutenant Nathan D. White, 30, Mesa, Arizona

APRIL 3
Marine Private First Class Chad E. Bales, 20, Coahoma, Texas
Army Sergeant Wilbert Davis, 40, Hinesville, Georgia
Marine Corporal Mark A. Evnin, 21, South Burlington, Vermont

Army Captain Edward J. Korn, 31, Savannah, Georgia
Army Staff Sergeant Nino D. Livaudais, 23, Ogden, Utah
Army Specialist Ryan P. Long, 21, Seaford, Delaware
Army Specialist Donald S. Oaks Jr., 20, Harborcreek, Pennsylvania
Army Sergeant First Class Randy Rehn, 36, Longmont, Colorado
Army Captain Russell B. Rippetoe, 27, Arvada, Colorado
Army Sergeant Todd J. Robbins, 33, Hart, Michigan
Marine Corporal Erik H. Silva, 23, Holtville, California

APRIL 4
Army Captain Tristan N. Aitken, 31, State College, Pennsylvania
Army Private First Class Wilfred D. Bellard, 20, Lake Charles, Louisiana
Army Specialist Daniel Francis J. Cunningham, 33, Lewiston, Maine
Marine Captain Travis Ford, 30, Oceanside, California
Marine Corporal Bernard G. Gooden, 22, Mount Vernon, New York
Army Private Devon D. Jones, 19, San Diego, California
Marine First Lieutenant Brian M. McPhillips, 25, Pembroke, Massachusetts
Marine Sergeant Duane R. Rios, 25, Griffith, Indiana
Marine Captain Benjamin Sammis, 29, Rehoboth, Massachusetts
Army Sergeant First Class Paul R. Smith, 33, Tampa, Florida

APRIL 5
Army Sergeant Stevon Booker, 34, Apollo, Pennsylvania
Army Specialist Larry K. Brown, 22, Jackson, Mississippi
Marine First Sergeant Edward Smith, 38, Vista, California

APRIL 6
Army Private First Class Gregory P. Huxley Jr., 19, Forestport, New York
Army Private Kelley S. Prewitt, 24, Birmingham, Alabama

Lance Corporal Ian Malone, Dublin, Ireland
Piper Christopher Muzvuru, United Kingdom
Fusilier Kelan J. Turrington, United Kingdom

APRIL 7
Marine Lance Corporal Andrew Julian Aviles, 18, Tampa, Florida
Air Force Captain Eric B. Das, 30, Amarillo, Texas
Army Staff Sergeant Lincoln Hollinsaid, 27, Malden, Illinois
Army Second Lieutenant Jeffrey J. Kaylor, 24, Clifton, Virginia
Marine Corporal Jesus Martin Antonio Medellin, 21, Fort Worth, Texas

Army Private First Class Anthony S. Miller, 19, San Antonio, Texas
Army Specialist George A. Mitchell, 35, Rawlings, Maryland
Air Force Major William R. Watkins III, 37, Danville, Virginia

APRIL 8
Army Corporal Henry L. Brown, 22, Natchez, Mississippi
Marine Private First Class Juan Guadalupe Garza, 20, Temperance, Michigan
Army Sergeant First Class John W. Marshall, 50, Los Angeles, California
Army Private First Class Jason M. Meyer, 23, Howell, Michigan
Air Force Staff Sergeant Scott D. Sather, 29, Clio, Michigan
Army Staff Sergeant Robert A. Stever, 36, Pendleton, Oregon

APRIL 10
Marine Gunnery Sergeant Jeff Bohr, 39, San Clemente, California
Army Staff Sergeant Terry W. Hemingway, 39, Willingboro, New Jersey

APRIL 11
Marine Staff Sergeant Riayan A. Tejeda, 26, New York, New York

APRIL 12
Marine Corporal Jesus A. Gonzalez, 22, Indio, California
Marine Lance Corporal David Edward Owens Jr., 20, Winchester, Virginia

APRIL 13
Army Specialist Gil Mercado, 25, Paterson, New Jersey

APRIL 14
Army Private Johnny Brown, 21, Troy, Alabama
Army Specialist Thomas Arthur Foley III, 23, Dresden, Tennessee
Marine Corporal Armando Ariel Gonzalez, 25, Hialeah, Florida
Army Specialist Richard A. Goward, 32, Midland, Michigan
Army Private First Class Joseph P. Mayek, 20, Rock Springs, Wyoming
Marine Corporal Jason David Mileo, 20, Centreville, Maryland

Journalists Who Died or Were Missing in Action During Combat in Operation Iraqi Freedom

MARCH 22–23

Terry Lloyd, ITV News correspondent

Paul Moran, freelancer on assignment for the Australian Broadcasting Corporation (ABC)

Fred Nerac, ITV News cameraman

Hussein Othman, ITV News translator

MARCH 30

Gaby Rado, Channel 4 News (U.K.)

APRIL 2

Kaveh Golestan, freelancer on assignment for the BBC

APRIL 3

Michael Kelly, editor, *Atlantic Monthly*, and columnist, *Washington Post*

APRIL 6

David Bloom, NBC News correspondent

Kamaran Abdurazaq Muhamed, BBC translator

APRIL 7

Christian Liebig, reporter for *Focus* (Germany)

Julio Anguita Parrado, reporter for *El Mundo* (Spain)

APRIL 8

Tareq Ayyoub, al-Jazeera

José Couso, Telecinco (Spain) cameraman

Taras Protsyuk, Reuters cameraman

APRIL 14

Veronica Cabrera, America TV (Argentina)

Mario Podestá, freelancer on assignment with America TV (Argentina)

ACKNOWLEDGMENTS

A t NBC News, nothing hits the air that doesn't bear the stamp of dozens of creative and dedicated broadcast professionals. The same holds true for this book and DVD, which would never have come into being without the collaborative efforts of numerous people from many different areas of the company. First of all, a special thanks is due to all the above NBC News and MSNBC personnel who generously shared their personal wartime experiences for this project. *Top row, left to right:* Jim Bruton, Bob Arnot, John Kooistra, Bob Lapp, Joe Klimovitz, Rob Grant, Chip Reid, John Zito, Sam Sambataro, Bill Angelucci, Sebastian Rich. *Bottom row, left to right:* Tom Aspell, Gerard Miller, Paul Nassar, David Bloom (pictured), Craig White, Dana Lewis, Lai Ling Jew, Kerry Sanders, Danny Miller. *Not pictured:* Tim Uehlinger. We would also like to thank our Telemundo colleagues who served as embedded journalists: Gustavo Mariel and Luz Elena Torres.

Just as essential were the many professionals who contributed their talents with unflagging grace and good humor in the face of a demanding production schedule. From NBC News: Phil Alongi; Don Bailey; Justin Balding; Stacy Brady; Robert Dembo; General Wayne Downing, retired; Melissa Dunlop; Fred Francis; Ben Goldstein; Leora Kahn; David Kay; Tony Koren; George Lewis; Mark Lukasiewicz; Samuel Mandragona; Rekha Matchanickal; General Barry McCaffrey, retired; David McCormick; Vice Admiral Dennis McGinn, retired; Elena Nachmanoff; Danny Noa; Sharon Scott; Robin Sherman; General Mike Short, retired; Erik Sorenson; Rita Sultana; David Verdi; Bill Wheatley; Bob Windrem. From NBC

Enterprises: April Brock, Kim Niemi, George Nunes, Ed Wilson. From Andrews McMeel Publishing: Holly Camerlinck, Michelle Daniel, Dorothy O'Brien, Christine Schillig. From *Army Magazine:* Mary French, Dennis Steele. From the NBC Agency: Stuart Myers, Omar Sanders. From NBC New Media: Jonathan Accarrino, Winston Johnson, David Ondrick, Collin Pisarra. From NBC Information Technology: Mike Alongi, Jayesh Bhatia; Dave Buono, Kaladhar Chandra; Cornelia Lin, Matt Maresco, Craig Murray, Jack Ng, Bonnie Optekman, Greg Palmes, Brian Perkins, Brendan Roche, Duval Trivedi; Jonathan Webb. From NBC Executive Communications: William Bartlett.

In addition, we would be remiss if we failed to acknowledge the contributions of the following people: Michelle Acevedo; Carol Aerenson; Meredith Ahr; Benita Alexander-Noel; Melanie Altarescu; Kelly Anderson; Diane Anello; Hannah Arkin; Rikki Arkin; Howard Averill; Loren Michelman Bandler; Robert Barnett; Kathy Bayer; Mike Benevento; Latrice Bennett; Melissa Biondi; Allan Bivona; Cameron Blanchard; Rosemary Bobay; Christopher Browne; Kathleen Butler; Ambassador Richard Butler; Alexis Camerlinck; Katherine Campbell; Sharon Campbell; Tessa Capodice; Steve Capus; Matt Carluccio; B. J. Carretta; Andy Cashman; Juju Chang; Alexa Chopivksy; Donna Cintorino; Rob Clarke; Aaron Clendening; Leah Cohen; Debra Colchamiro; Ronnie Coppola; Jocelyn Cordova; David Corvo; David Coventry; Matt Crockett; Fran Cunningham; Maryanne DeCandia; Nilsa Delacruz; Joseph Depierro; Nick D'Errico; Greg Doyle; Claire Duffy; Ann Dunlop; Leslie Duong; Dick Ebersol; Mark Effron; Bob Epstein; Hart Faber; Scott Feinstein; Dianne Festa; Ada Famulari; Mike Farris; William Fenick; Jamitha Fields; Dexter Filkins; M. L. Flynn; Tony Franqueira; Joseph Gabriel; Jim Gaines; Roxanne Garcia; Jim Gerety; Leslie Gimbel; Peter Giordano; Lawnie Grant; Chris Hansen; Bill Hartnett; Colonel Arthur Haubold; Mike Heimbuch; James Hill; Brett Holey; Blair Holman; Julie Holstein; Jon Hookstratten; Lisa Hsia; Angie Hu; Lieutenant Colonel Samuel Hudspath; Jim Idiart; Stacey Irvin; Bob Jensen; D. J. Johnson; Dottie Johnson; Kyle Kaino; Ken Kalthoff; Lee Kamlet; Joannie Kaplan; Michael Karp; Tom Keenan; Loretta Kraft; Nate Kravis; Sam Kravis; Talia Kravis; Alison Kubaska; Lewis Kuo; Tammy Kupperman; Alex Kyriacou; Donna Leach; Aimee Leone; Barbara Levin; Dave Levine; John Libretto; Jay Linden; David Lipsius; David Lyons; Christopher Madden; Doug Maio; Sumit Mathur; Christi Mayer; Laurie McCall; Erin McCarron; Thomas McGarry; Mary Ann Meigs; Olivia Metzger; Joe Michaels; Jim Miklaszewski; Jim Mills; Colonel Alvina Mitchell; Kimberly Morgan; Dennis Murphy; Mike Nardi; Don Nash; Jennifer Novick; Beth O'Connell; Abby Oppenheim; Felicia Patinkin; Sara Perkowski; Otto Petersen; General Dan Petrosky, retired; Jerry Petry; Rear Admiral Stephen Pietropaoli; Zinta Poilovs; Rich Pruefer; Vladimir Rabinovich; Frank Radice; Meaghan Rady; Brigadier General Ronald Rand; Kevin Roff; Lindsay Rovegno; Victoria Rubin; Alan Seiffert; Jared Shapiro; Saul Shapiro; Lloyd Siegel; Justin Smith; Susan Sullivan; Bambi Tascarella; Tom Touchet; Carmela Tripodi; Jim Vidakovich; David Wells; Ron Wilson; Eric Wishnie.

PHOTO CREDITS

Unless otherwise specified, copyright on the works reproduced lies with the respective photographers and agencies. Despite extensive research, it has not always been possible to establish ownership. Where this is the case, please notify the publisher and we will be pleased to make corrections to future editions.

p. iii: AP/Wide World Photos; p. vii: AP Wide World Photos; p. ix: Christopher Anderson/VII; p. x: NBC NEWS; p. xi: Robert Nickelsberg/Getty Images; p. xvii: Simon Walker/Reuters; p. xviii: USAF; p. 1: Gamma; p. 2: *left:* NBC NEWS; *right:* USN; p. 3: Todd Plitt; p. 4: *top:* Bill Arkin; *lower left and right:* Space Imaging Middle East; p. 5: *top:* USAF; *bottom:* NBC NEWS; pp 6–7: USN; p. 8: *top:* USAF *bottom:* USN; p. 9: *all:* USN; p. 10: *top:* USN *bottom:* USAF; p. 11: *top:* USAF; *bottom:* Eric Draper/WH/KRT; pp. 12–13: Christopher Anderson/VII; p. 14: *top:* AP/Wide World Photos; *bottom:* Joe Raedle/Getty Images; p. 15: *top:* Eric Feferberg/AFP/Getty; *bottom:* Robert Nickelsberg/Getty Images; pp. 16–17: Benjamin Lowy/Corbis; p. 18: Dennis Steele/*Army Magazine;* p. 19: AP/Wide World Photos; p. 20: Paul Nassar/NBC NEWS; p. 21: Craig White/NBC NEWS; p. 22: *top:* Bob Lapp/NBC NEWS; *middle:* Dennis Steele/*Army Magazine; bottom left:* Craig White/NBC NEWS; *bottom right:* Bob Lapp/NBC NEWS; p. 23: NBC NEWS; p. 24: *right:* Paul Nassar/NBC NEWS; *left:* Roger Shuck/3rd Infantry Division/USA; p. 25: *top left:* Sebastian Rich/NBC NEWS; *top right:* Sebastian Rich/NBC NEWS; *lower right:* Danny Miller/NBC NEWS; *lower left:* Sebastian Rich/NBC NEWS; p. 26: *all:* Bill Angelucci/NBC NEWS; p. 27: *top left:* John Zito/NBC NEWS; *top right:* Chip Reid/NBC NEWS; *lower right:* Joe Klimovitz/NBC NEWS; *lower left:* John Zito/NBC NEWS; p. 28: *top:* John Zito/NBC NEWS; *bottom:* Bill Angelucci/NBC NEWS; p. 29: *all:* Bill Angelucci/NBC NEWS; p. 30: Todd Plitt; p. 31: Todd Plitt; p. 32: *all:* 10th Special Forces Group; p. 33: USAF; p. 34: *top:* 10th Special Forces Group; *bottom:* N. Cepeda/*San Diego Union Tribune;* p. 35: *all:* 10th Special Forces Group; p. 36: Cho Sungsu/Gamma; p. 37: *top:* USMC; *bottom:* Faleh Kheiber/Reuters; p. 38: Bob Lapp/NBC NEWS; p. 39: *left:* Justin Balding/NBC NEWS; *right:* NBC NEWS; pp. 40–41: AP/Wide World Photos; p. 42: *top:* MLRS/Lockheed Martin; *bottom:* DOD; p. 43: *top:* UK MOD; *bottom:* Bill Angelucci/NBC NEWS; pp. 44–45: AP/Wide World Photos; p. 46: *all:* USAF; p. 47: *top:* Ramzi Haidar/Getty *bottom:* NBC NEWS; pp. 48–49: AP/Wide World Photos; p. 50: *top left:* Carolyn Cole/*L.A. Times; top right:* STR/Reuters; *bottom:* USMC; p. 51: Bruce Adams/Reuters; p. 52: Benjamin Lowy/Corbis; p. 53: *left:* Fakh Kheiber/Reuters; *right, all:* al-Jazeera; p. 54: USAF; p. 55: James Hill; p. 56: *top left:* NBC NEWS; *middle left:* NBC NEWS; *bottom left:* NBC NEWS; *bottom right:* Paul Nassar/NBC NEWS; p. 57: Romeo Gacad/AFP/Getty Images; pp. 58–59: Kai Pfaffenbach/Reuters; pp. 60–61: James Hill; p. 62: *top:* USAF; *bottom:* AP/Wide World Photos; p. 63: *top:* David Leeson/*Dallas Morning News; bottom:* Peter Andrews/Reuters; p. 64: Ron Haviv/VII; p. 65: Patrick Baz/AFP/Getty Images; p. 66: *top:* Stuart Myers/NBC NEWS; *middle:* Sebastian Rich/NBC NEWS; *bottom:* Joe Raedle/Getty Images; p. 67: *all:* Sebastian Rich/NBC NEWS; p. 68: Eric Feferberg/AFP/Getty Images; p. 69: Justin Balding/NBC NEWS; p. 70: *all:* Justin Balding/NBC NEWS; p. 71: Justin Balding/NBC NEWS; p. 72: Justin Balding/NBC NEWS; p. 73: UK MOD; pp. 74–75: Robert Nickelsberg/Getty Images; p. 76: Palmour Hayne/*NC Times*/Gamma; p. 77: AP/Wide World Photos; p. 78: Stuart Myers/NBC NEWS; p. 79: NBC NEWS; p. 80: *top:* USN; *bottom:* DOD; p. 81: NBC NEWS; pp. 82–83: Benjamin Lowy/Corbis; p. 84: *top:* Nicholas Roberts/AFP/Getty Images; *bottom:* NBC NEWS; p. 85: *top:* Lara Sukhtian; *bottom:* Unknown; p. 86: *top:* Ilkka Uimonen/Magnum; *bottom:* MSNBC; p. 87: AP/Wide World Photos; p. 88: Sebastian Rich/NBC NEWS; p. 89: USN; p. 90: *top:* USA; *bottom:* Peter Turnley/Corbis; p. 91: *top:* Russell Boyce/Reuters; *bottom:* Jon Mills/Pool/Reuters; p. 92: AFP/Getty Images; p. 93: Robert Nickelsberg/Getty Images; p. 94: Robert Nickelsberg/Getty Images; p. 95: *all:* Bill Angelucci/NBC NEWS; pp. 96–97: Kuni Takahashi/*Boston Herald*/Reflex; p. 98: *top:* David Gilkey/*Detroit Free Press*/KRT; *bottom:* Peter Turnley/Corbis; p. 99: Sebastian

Rich/NBC NEWS; p. 100: *top:* Ian Jones/Gamma; *bottom:* John Zito/NBC NEWS; p. 101: *top right:* NBC NEWS; *bottom right:* Gerry Miller/ NBC NEWS; p. 102: 10th Special Forces Group; p. 103: *top:* UK MOD; *right:* USMC; p. 104: John Zito/NBC NEWS; p. 105: John Zito/NBC NEWS; p. 106: *top left:* AP/Wide World Photos; *bottom left:* Bill Angelucci/NBC NEWS; p. 107: Lara Sukhtian; p. 108: *all:* Joseph Giordano/*Stars and Stripes*; p. 109: *top:* Ilkka Uimonen/Magnum Photos; *bottom:* AP/Wide World Photos; p. 110: USA; p. 111: Tim Sloan/AFP/Getty; p. 112: USN; p. 113: 10th Special Forces Group; pp. 114–115: Bartholomew/NBC; p. 116: *top left:* Bill Arkin; *middle left:* DOD; *bottom left:* DOD; *bottom right:* Thomas Hartwell/USAID; p. 117: Goran Tomasevic/Reuters; p. 118: *top:* Centcom; *bottom:* DOD; p. 119: USN; p. 120: *top:* Staff Sergeant Matthew Hannen; *bottom:* USAF; p. 121: USN; p. 122: *top:* Cho Sungsu/Gamma; *bottom left:* Captain Gregory R. "Irish" deMik; *bottom right:* Goran Tomasevic/Reuters; p. 123: *top:* NBC NEWS; *bottom:* USN; p. 124: *top:* USMC; *bottom:* USAF; p. 125: Iraqi TV; p. 126: Dennis Steele/*Army Magazine*; p. 127: *top:* Frederic LaFargue/Gamma; *bottom:* Unknown; p. 128: AP/Wide World Photos; p. 129: Dennis Steele/*Army Magazine*; p. 130: John Zito/NBC NEWS; p. 131: *top:* Stuart Myers/NBC NEWS; *bottom right:* NBC NEWS; pp. 132–133: Rob Curtis/Army Times/Corbis; p. 134: *top left:* Bill Angelucci/NBC NEWS; *top right:* NBC NEWS; *bottom:* MSNBC; p. 135: *top:* MSNBC; *bottom:* John Zito/NBC NEWS; p. 136: *all:* NBC NEWS; p. 138: Kerry Sanders/NBC NEWS; p. 139: John Zito/NBC NEWS; p. 140: *top:* Centcom; *bottom:* Centcom; p. 141: Centcom; p. 142: Sebastian Rich/NBC NEWS; p. 143: John Zito/NBC NEWS; p. 144: Sebastian Rich/NBC NEWS; p. 145: Lara Sukhtian; p. 146: *top:* Michael Perez/*Philadelphia Inquirer*/KRT; *bottom:* Bob Houlihan/Corbis; p. 147: *top:* Chris Bouroncle/Corbis; *bottom:* Bill Angelucci/NBC NEWS; p. 148: *top:* Hayne Palmour/Gamma; *bottom:* Sebastian Rich/NBC NEWS; p. 149: David Leeson/ *Dallas Morning News;* pp. 150–151: Jim Watson/Corbis; p. 152: *top:* Romeo Gacad/Corbis; *bottom:* Christopher Anderson/VII; p. 153: Sebastian Rich/NBC NEWS; p. 154: Robert Nickelsberg/Getty Images; p. 155: Bill Angelucci/NBC NEWS; p. 156: David Gilkey/*Detroit Free Press*/KRT; p. 157: Patrick Baz/AFP/Corbis; p. 158: *top:* Patrick Baz/AFP/Corbis; *bottom:* Bill Angelucci/NBC NEWS; p. 159: *left:* Bill Angelucci/NBC NEWS; *right:* Sebastian Rich/NBC NEWS; p. 160: Master Sergeant Keith Reed; p. 161: *left bottom:* Sebastian Rich/NBC NEWS; *top right:* NBC NEWS; p. 162: Sebastian Rich/NBC NEWS; p. 163: *top:* Kerry Sanders/NBC NEWS; *bottom:* Stuart Myers/NBC NEWS; p. 165: Dennis Steele/*Army Magazine*; p. 166: *top:* Gloria Ferniz/San Antonio Express/Zuma Press; *bottom:* Sandy Huffaker/Getty Images; p. 167: *top:* Bill Pugliano/Getty Images; *bottom:* Jeff Siner/*Charlotte Observer*; pp. 168–174: Dennis Steele/*Army Magazine*; p. 175: Bartholomew/NBC; p. 176: *top:* Jack Gruber/*USA Today*; *bottom:* Jack Gruber/*USA Today*; p. 177: *top:* John Carrington/*Savannah Morning News*; *bottom:* AP/Wide World Photos; p. 178: *top:* AP/Wide World Photos; *bottom:* NBC NEWS; p. 179: Bartholomew/NBC; p. 180: *top:* Scott Nelson/Getty Images; *bottom:* Justin Balding/NBC NEWS.; p. 181: *top:* NBC NEWS; *bottom:* David Dismukes; p. 182: *left:* Fred Scott/BBC; *right:* AP/Wide World Photos; p. 183: *left:* AP/Wide World Photos; *right:* AP/Wide World Photos; p. 184: *top:* Buu Alain/Gamma; *bottom:* Dennis Steele/*Army Magazine*; p. 185: USAF; p. 186: *top:* LaFargue Frederic/Gamma; *bottom:* Dennis Steele/*Army Magazine*; p. 187: Dennis Steele/*Army Magazine*; p. 188: *top:* Goran Tomasevic/Reuters; *bottom:* AP/Wide World Photos; p. 189: *top:* David Dismukes; *bottom:* Bahnram Mark Sobhami/*San Antonio Express*; p. 190: AP/Wide World Photos; p. 191: Ron Haviv/VII; p. 192: *top:* David Leeson/ *Dallas Morning News; bottom:* NBC NEWS; p. 193: Faleh Kheiber/Reuters; p. 194: *top:* 10th Special Forces Group; *bottom:* NBC NEWS; p. 195: NBC NEWS; p. 196: Cho Sungsu/Gamma; p. 197: *top:* AP/Wide World Photos; *bottom:* James Hill; p. 198: Dennis Steele/*Army Magazine*; p. 199: *top:* Peters Andrew/Reuters; *bottom:* Bassignac Gilles/Gamma; p. 200: AP/Wide World Photos; p. 201: *top:* Lara Sukhtian; *bottom:* Justin Balding/NBC NEWS; p. 202: *top:* Lara Sukhtian; *bottom:* Patrick Baz/AFP/Corbis; p. 203: AP/Wide World Photos; p. 204: *top:* Carolyn Cole/LAT; *bottom:* AP/Wide World Photos; p. 205: *top:* Rick Loomis/LAT; *bottom:* Unknown; p. 206: Jeff Siner/*Charlotte Observer*; p. 207: USMC; p. 208: *top:* Meyer/*Dallas Morning News; bottom:* Andrade Patrick/Gamma; p. 209: John Carrington/*Savannah Morning News*; pp. 210–211: AP/Wide World Photos; p. 212: Unknown; p. 213: David Gilkey/*Detroit Free Press*/KRT; pp. 214–215: Centcom; p. 216: *all:* AP/Wide World Photos; p. 217: *top:* Dennis Steele/*Army Magazine; bottom:* Rick Loomis/LAT; pp. 218–219: Sebastian Rich/NBC NEWS; p. 220: Jim Barcus/*Kansas City Star*; p. 221: *top:* Centcom; *bottom:* Travis Heying/*Wichita Eagle*/KRT; p. 222: Dennis Steele/*Army Magazine*; p. 223: USN; p. 224: Kuni Takahashi/*Boston Herald*/Reflex News; p. 225: Christopher Anderson/VII; p. 235: Rob Clark